Growing from Infancy to Adulthood

CURRENT PROBLEMS IN EDUCATION

Edited by WILLIAM H. BURTON

THE USE OF INSTRUCTIONAL MATERIALS
   By Amo de Bernardis, *Portland, Oregon, Public Schools*

UNDERSTANDING MENTALLY RETARDED CHILDREN
   By Harriet E. Blodgett and Grace J. Warfield, *The Sheltering Arms, Minneapolis*

GROWING FROM INFANCY TO ADULTHOOD
   By Edward C. Britton and J. Merritt Winans, *Sacramento State College*

IMPROVING THE ARITHMETIC PROGRAM
   By Leo J. Brueckner, *formerly University of Minnesota*

COUNSELING IN THE PHYSICAL EDUCATION PROGRAM
   By Rosalind Cassidy, *University of California, Los Angeles*

APPROACHES TO INDIVIDUALIZED READING
   By Helen Fisher Darrow and Virgil M. Howes, *San Diego County Department of Education*

THE ELEMENTARY SCHOOL CHILD AND HIS POSTURE PATTERNS
   By Evelyn A. Davies, *Indiana University*

ADMINISTRATIVE THEORY
   By Daniel E. Griffiths, *Teachers College, Columbia University*

WORKSHOPS FOR TEACHERS
   By Mary A. O'Rourke, *Massachusetts State Teachers College at Salem*, and William H. Burton, *formerly Harvard University*

IMPROVING READING IN THE JUNIOR HIGH SCHOOL
   By L. Jane Stewart, Frieda H. Heller, and Elsie J. Alberty, *The University School, The Ohio State University*

THE ADMINISTRATOR AND THE IMPROVEMENT OF READING
   By Ruth Strang and Donald M. Lindquist, *Teachers College, Columbia University*

CREATIVITY IN THE ELEMENTARY SCHOOL
   By Miriam E. Wilt, *Temple University*

HELPING TEACHERS UNDERSTAND PRINCIPALS
   By Wilbur A. Yauch, *Northern Illinois University*

Growing from Infancy to Adulthood

A SUMMARY OF THE CHANGING CHARACTERISTICS OF
CHILDREN AND YOUTH

by

Edward C. Britton

and

J. Merritt Winans

BOTH OF SACRAMENTO STATE COLLEGE

ILLUSTRATIONS BY GLEN DINES

NEW YORK

APPLETON-CENTURY-CROFTS, INC.

Copyright © 1958 by
APPLETON-CENTURY-CROFTS, INC.

All rights reserved. This book, or parts thereof, must not be reproduced in any form without permission of the publisher.

636-6

LIBRARY OF CONGRESS CARD NUMBER: 58-7149

Test edition copyright, 1956, by
Edward C. Britton and J. Merritt Winans

PRINTED IN THE UNITED STATES OF AMERICA
E-13203

Preface

This handbook offers a convenient summary of the typical patterns of children's behavior at each of six stages from infancy to adulthood. The first chapter reviews briefly some of the general questions related to organizing behavior into characteristics. The language throughout is non-technical and the material is planned for quick reference.

The material was prepared in the belief that it might be useful or even indispensable for several groups of readers.

1. For parents, the book
   Helps achieve an understanding of the reason for children's behavior,
   Leads to more reasonable expectations of the behavior of children,
   Stimulates a keener observation of children,
   Provides a sound basis for guiding children's growth, and
   Enables anticipation of the forthcoming stages in children's behavior.
2. For teachers, leaders, and administrators in all types of schools and community agencies, the book
   Enables a fitting of curriculum, programs, materials, and lesson plans to the needs, interests, and capacities of children,
   Provides help in understanding and assisting the child with a behavior problem,
   Helps the teacher moving to a new grade level and the beginning student-teacher to prepare ahead of time,
   Provides a reference during parent-teacher conferences and follow-up reading for parents later.
3. For students in courses in growth and development, guidance, methods, and other education courses, the book
   Leads to understanding of children's characteristics fundamental to such courses,
   Facilitates a review of course material,

Assists in the observation of children, and
Serves as a text or collateral reading.
4. For children and youth, the book
Gives insights into their own behavior otherwise not ordinarily obtainable.

Previously the only available book at all comparable to this in objective and scope was one written before 1946. The present work is considerably more comprehensive, includes the extensive research of the past eleven years, is organized in more usable form, and includes an overview chapter and annotated references to the literature and film resources.

In preparation of this book, the authors reviewed several hundred reports and summaries of research. The statements offered in this book are the result of a critical analysis of these sources and a selection of significant items about which there is substantial agreement.

The book in preliminary form has been used by parents and by college students in courses during several semesters. These readers have verified the generalizations in the book by checking them against youngsters observed in the classroom or in the family. It was their enthusiastic comments that encouraged the authors to prepare the material for wider distribution.

The writers wish to express their appreciation to the illustrator, Mr. Glen Dines, who combined a keen interest in the subject matter, patient and constructive help in many hours of conference, and artistic talents that speak for themselves.

Thanks are due also to colleagues of the writers for assistance and suggestions, especially Dr. Mildred Dawson, who helped in planning the book and preparing a first draft of Chapters 2 and 3, and Dr. Harry Aron, who offered many useful suggestions and criticisms on Chapters 2 through 7.

With a view to improving this handbook in possible future revisions, the authors invite observations, suggestions, and criticisms.

Recognizing that a dedication is pretentious for a work of this scope, the authors nevertheless would like to say that they always had in mind Gail, Laurie, Douglas, and Gordon, who show how all children are the same and yet differ one from the other. Finally, the authors are pondering the implications of the statement made by one youthful critic after reading sections of *Growing from Infancy to Adulthood:* "Gee, this stuff is wonderful. When can we get the low-down on parents?"

E.C.B.
J.M.W.

Contents

Preface v

1. All Children Are the Same; Each One Is Different 1
2. Characteristics of Children in Infancy
   (The First Five Years) 21
3. Characteristics of Children in Early Childhood
   (Ages 6, 7, and 8) 33
4. Characteristics of Children in Later Childhood
   (Ages: Boys 9, 10, and 11; Girls 9 and 10) 46
5. Characteristics of Preadolescence
   (Ages: Boys 12 and 13; Girls 11 and 12) 58
6. Characteristics of Children in Early Adolescence
   (Ages: Boys 14, 15, and 16; Girls 13, 14, and 15) 68
7. Late Adolescence
   (Ages: Boys 17 through 20; Girls 16 through 20) 85

Appendix   I. Percentiles for Weight and Height of American Children 92
           II. Chronology of Pubertal Developments in Height, Weight, and Sex Characteristics 94
           III. Textbooks on Child Development 96
           IV. Reports and Summaries of Research on Child Development 101
           V. General Books, Pamphlets, and Journals on Child Development 104
           VI. Films on Child Development 110

Index 115

1

All Children Are the Same; Each One Is Different

TO WHAT EXTENT ARE ALL CHILDREN THE SAME?

This booklet rests on the assumption that children pass through a series of well-defined stages, each with its typical patterns of behavior. It is true that these patterns are subject to exceptions and do not apply to minute details and variations of behavior. Yet to the expert observer there are striking similarities in the behaviors of each age, enabling sufficiently detailed and concrete descriptions to be highly useful to all who seek to understand children. To this extent it is reasonable to say that "all children are the same."

WHAT IS THE EVIDENCE THAT "ALL CHILDREN ARE THE SAME"?

The knowledge about the sameness of children comes from the precise, objective, carefully-recorded observations of children and youth made by research workers over the past sixty years. The outstanding pioneer and probably the major contributor to knowledge about the age-graded behavior characteristics of children is Dr. Arnold Gesell, who founded the Yale Institute of Human Development in 1911. His writings, beginning with reports in 1925, reached a peak with his well-known *Child Development,* appearing in the 1940's, and finally with *Youth, the Years from Ten to Sixteen,* published in 1956.

In spite of substantial criticisms, shortly to be mentioned, Gesell's books have deserved their wide popularity among teachers and parents. They are based on minute, voluminous observations of children under conditions of scientific exactness, and are written in clear, useful form.

In the past two or more decades, other centers of research on child and youth development have been making, directly or indirectly, major contributions to present knowledge about the ways in which all children are the same. These centers include the Iowa Child Welfare Research Station, Rockefeller Institutes of Child Welfare (now under the General Education Board), and many universities, notably California, Columbia, Harvard, and Stanford.

New insights have been reached because the long-range programs of these research centers have enabled use of the longitudinal approach: the continuous observation of the same individual children over a period of years. This method has been much more effective than the cross-sectional approach in which large numbers are surveyed at one time, such as in a comparison of groups of six-, seven-, and eight-year-olds. Significant facts are concealed in the averaging that must take place in the latter approach.

Further evidence of the similarities in behavior patterns of children at each age comes from investigations of life in American communities made by sociologists such as Lloyd W. Warner, Allison Davis, and Robert J. Havighurst, and also from studies of life in primitive societies made by Margaret Mead and other anthropologists.

A new source of evidence is the nation-wide surveys of adolescents, based on personal interviews and written responses, which have been completed and made available in the past two years.

An example of current research of potential significance is that being conducted by Cecil V. Millard in the Child Development Laboratory at Michigan State University. He is looking for "growth relationships in individual height, mental, and reading curves." Should these be established with the mathematical exactness he anticipates, it would be possible to say, for example, that a child is ready to begin reading when he reaches a certain percentage of his full adult height (61 per cent is indicated in Millard's preliminary studies).

Research on children and youth suffers from limitations which must be recognized. Gesell's findings on early teen-agers, for example, were based primarily on 115 youngsters, definitely above average in intelligence and in economic class, all living in one community. His interpretations also suffer from the attempt to subdivide behavior patterns into too many levels, so that the sharp distinctions, as between the behavior of the five-and the five-and-one-half-year-old, or the twelve-and the thirteen-year-old, do not seem to be justified.

Other kinds of limitations of available research are reviewed later in this chapter under the heading, "How to Interpret Chapters 2 Through 7."

To summarize, it may be said that with due allowance for limitations of existing research, there is an impressively large and increasing amount of evidence indicating the existence of many important similarities in the behavior patterns of children at various ages. These similarities are recognized and included to a varying extent in current texts, books for parents, and other books about child and youth development. Chapters 2 to 7 set forth these characteristics in a complete, conveniently organized form.

WHAT FORCES MAKE CHILDREN THE SAME?

As members of Homo sapiens children have many important physical similarities. The growth of children follows a common "biological time table," even though there are late and early arrivals. Appendix I shows the steady increases in weight and height, and Appendix II the lesser uniformity in development of sex characteristics. Both are under the direction of inherited forces.

The environment is the other force contributing to the sameness of children. The home, the community, and the nation are crucial in the child's development. Society molds its members, young and old, into a sameness. With television, mass higher education, and a leveling of family income, our culture may be moving toward more unified values and behaviors.

The importance of social pressures in developing the characteristics of children has also been recognized by sociologists in the term *developmental tasks*. Robert J. Havighurst, who first used the term to characterize the stages through which children pass, says: "A developmental task is a task which arises at or about a certain period in the life of the individual, successful achievement of which leads to his happiness and to success with later tasks, while failure leads to unhappiness in the individual, disapproval by the society, and difficulty with later tasks." For example, a developmental task of adolescence is "Achieving new and more mature relations with age mates of both sexes." This task is based on both the developing physical characteristics of the adolescent and the demands made upon him in his society. Havighurst's contribution lies in emphasizing the influence of society in determining the changing nature of children, and in helping parents and teachers to be aware of the many new conditions to which the growing child must adjust. In a real sense the child's "characteristics" are his responses to "developmental tasks." Heredity and environment establish developmental tasks; heredity and environment determine characteristics.

OF WHAT VALUE TO ADULTS IS KNOWING HOW "ALL CHILDREN ARE THE SAME"?

Teaching is efficient when based upon insight into the pupil being taught. This insight is dependent upon an understanding of the characteristics of all children at that age. The importance of this understanding is illustrated by pupil *readiness*. There is convincing evidence that children can learn effectively only when they are physically, emotionally, and intellectually ready. At six years, the teaching of chronological events in history is a waste of time. The typical child in the first grade may memorize dates but they have little or no meaning for him. He may acquire the habit of saying things without understanding. He may also develop poor work attitudes and habits because of the inevitable frustration. Creativity and intellectual curiosity may be stunted. He becomes used to failure. The informed teacher is aware of the need for developing readiness and will give the pupil learning experiences appropriate to his maturity. He is aware of the child's expanding interests and is able to motivate him effectively. He knows the right time to lead the children into each learning.

The teacher who knows the changing characteristics of growing children is able to help them with social as well as intellectual adjustments. He knows their maturing attitudes to peers, parents, and other adults. He can spot irritating but temporary behaviors which children will discard in the normal course of events. He is also able to identify the kinds of behavior which indicate present and probably future maladjustment.

Of what value to parents is this information? According to those who read this book in draft form such knowledge is of great value. Their comments showed first a sense of relief. Parents tend to have unreal expectations of their children. The fact that "they are just like other kids" is a reassuring discovery, even though they may intend to do something about it. A further satisfaction grows out of discovering the child's real motives. The somewhat bewildered parent of the thirteen-year-old who spends most of his time with other children feels better knowing that this is not a rejection of the parent but rather indicates the child's typical and proper desire to establish himself with his peers and gain independence. The parent then understands and is pleased that his child is growing normally. He may allow the garage or part of the yard to be taken over as a meeting place so that this developmental step may be taken under some indirect supervision. The mother of the young baby learns that the child must achieve complete dependence and security before he moves on to acquire independence. She therefore responds to his every need through the first few months knowing that this attention will lay the emotional foundation for later self-reliance.

TO WHAT EXTENT IS EACH CHILD DIFFERENT?

Though this book is about the similarities among children it must look briefly at differences. One without the other would present an unbalanced picture. A review of differences throws light on similarities.

Each child is unique. Like a leaf on a tree, there never has been and never will be a duplicate. The idea of uniqueness among children is well recognized, but the extent of the differences may not be.

An example of differences is variation in weight. Appendix I shows a range of 46 pounds between the lightest and the heaviest 10 per cent of boys at age sixteen. Differences in timing of sexual maturity are illustrated by the fact, taken from Appendix II, that 3 out of 100 girls menstruate before age eleven and a like number at age sixteen or later. In health and soundness of body the differences are extreme, from the near perfection of the star athlete to the many deficiencies of the military reject. To health differences may be added variations of body build, skin and hair color, and physical attractiveness.

Intelligence test results show dramatic differences among children. About 10 per cent score an IQ of 80 or below, and have small chance of becoming competent in the subject matter of a typical elementary school. The highest 10 per cent score an IQ of 125 or above, and have adequate capacity for the most difficult kinds of specialized education leading to higher degrees.

An important but commonly unrecognized difference is that although two children may have the same IQ, one may rank high, let us say, in numerical and spatial abilities and low in verbal, while the other may have a different combination of high's and low's.

Scores measuring scholastic proficiency vary almost as much as intelligence scores. Children in the fourth year in elementary

ALL CHILDREN SAME; EACH DIFFERENT

schools in New York City were found to range in achievement levels, including reading, from ages six to sixteen.

Still other kinds of differences in interests, attitudes, and abilities, though not so well measured, can be assumed to be fully as great.

Children vary in the extent to which their emotional needs are met. Need for love, security, belonging, status, success, and independence are commonly identified. The range in emotional health is from the well-adjusted child to the one in the mental hospital.

Differences in social relationships are as numerous and important as those already mentioned. Consider, for example, the adolescent with many casual and several intimate friends, as contrasted with the youth who has none at all.

Whether we consider social or emotional traits, or, more broadly, all the aspects of personality, wide differences are the rule.

WHAT FORCES MAKE EACH CHILD DIFFERENT?

To the extent that either heredity or environment differs, children will be different. Even within the same family, heredity just as certainly causes differences among children (except for identical twins) as it causes similarity.

The most obvious and pronounced contribution of heredity is to variations in the physical structure and closely related traits, such as physique, hair color, and, to a somewhat lesser extent, stamina and physical co-ordination. The extent to which heredity accounts for differences in intelligence test scores is admittedly large though impossible to estimate with any accuracy. It might be mentioned in passing that these scores, contrary to popular impression, are also strongly influenced by environmental differences. Heredity establishes a ceiling on performance, environment determines how close to it the individual comes.

The contribution of heredity to personality characteristics can not be overlooked, even though it is both smaller and less obvious than to physical and intellectual traits.

Sociologists have stressed the role of society in developing uniformity in the characteristics of growing children. They also point out with equal emphasis the wide differences in behavior arising from the different sub-classes within the larger society. Lloyd Warner identified variations in child behavior characteristics for each of the six social classes in one community. Others have made similar analyses of other communities. Havighurst has shown the disparities in developmental tasks of different socio-economic classes.

Each child within the family has a different environment. The hidden, psychological differences may be more potent than the variations obvious to the casual outside observer. A child may be not wanted, or of the "wrong" sex, or over-protected, or be the buffer between discordant parents. The environment of the first-born is different from that of the last.

Besides differences in family relationships and social class, the child is influenced by differences in school, neighborhood, and region, and in political, religious, and ethnic backgrounds.

The growing conclusion among all social scientists is that areas of behavior once thought to be inborn or "natural" are really a product of the environment. Margaret Mead, for example, has pointed out that the basic attitudes of masculinity and femininity are learned and vary from place to place. The common elements in the American environment give all children many characteristics in common. The wide differences among

ALL CHILDREN SAME; EACH DIFFERENT

and within the many subgroups contribute to extensive individual differences.

OF WHAT VALUE IS KNOWLEDGE OF THE WAYS IN WHICH CHILDREN ARE DIFFERENT?

Knowledge of the many ways children differ provides as much insight into their behavior as does knowledge of similarities.

One of the teacher's major tasks is motivating children. Most pupils in any grade have interests in common. However, their varying socio-economic backgrounds strongly influence the form of these interests. For example, the teacher, incorrectly assuming that all of his pupils have middle-class aspirations, may point out to them the vocational advantages of learning algebra. Boys who are taught at home that physical and perhaps hazardous work is the only proper occupation for a real man will probably be little impressed. If he would be effective, the teacher learns about these cultural differences in values and behaviors.

The teacher who looks for the uniqueness in each child is able to establish rapport with him. As he learns the special characteristics of the pupil he learns how to communicate with him efficiently. The teacher knows the pupil's special interests, fears, limitations, and strengths. This knowledge, along with a warm acceptance of children, enables the teacher to gain the child's confidence.

The parent who studies the unique nature of each child enjoys advantages as does the teacher. Such parents will not expect each child to have the strengths of the most-approved child. They will appreciate the strengths of all as they see each as being unique. The adult, teacher or parent, who can see the special characteristics of each child he is with is able to behave more intelligently and effectively.

WHAT GENERAL PRINCIPLES ARE BASIC TO GROWTH AND DEVELOPMENT?

Researchers have tentatively identified some broad principles that appear to govern growth and development. The principles already implied in this chapter and those that follow below will provide useful preparation for reading Chapters 2 through 7.

Behavior Develops from Generalized to Specific Responses

Behaviors appear first in gross, simplified, over-all form and eventually become refined, differentiated, and specific. Early attempts at dancing, for example, are a crude involvement of the whole body. Later the child is able to move an arm or leg while holding the rest of the body still. This sequence is most evident as babies move from uncontrolled, over-all activity in response to an attractive object, to later controlled reaching and grasping.

The attitude of one child toward another begins as complete approval or disapproval in all-or-none fashion. Eventually he learns to like different people for different reasons or on different occasions. Growing refinement and discrimination characterize all aspects of development.

Over the Long Run Development Is Forward and Continuous

Seen at long range development moves steadily forward. The presence of some behavior does not imply that it will continue as a life-long habit. The child who fidgets and swings his legs at the dinner table is not in danger of doing it as an adult. Little boys often want to marry their mothers, but they move on to more mature attitudes. Even without parental guidance, and sometimes better without it, they advance. The principle is not invariable. For children to become fixed in a rut is possible but is far less likely than it seems to the worried parent.

ALL CHILDREN SAME; EACH DIFFERENT

Over Short Periods Growth Appears Irregular

"Two steps forward and one back," appears to be the pattern. The two-year-old who is doing well with toilet training has lapses. The seven-year-old who usually sets the table sometimes forgets, or dawdles, or rebels. The independent seventeen-year-old who insists on setting his own course sometimes needs the parental guidance and comforting reassurance usually reserved for his younger brother or sister. The teacher often observes rapid growth in reading followed by a long plateau.

Another factor leading to the irregularity of growth curve over short periods is the child's tendency to acquire new skills and ideas in exaggerated form. He overdoes it. When he first learns independence he is very negative. When he first learns "mine" he is completely selfish. As he gains assurance with these new characteristics he modifies them to suitable proportions. In a similar manner does his father acquire new skills in golf.

Various Aspects of Growth Are Inter-related.

It is commonly observed that different kinds of development are co-ordinate. The child who is tall for his age will probably be one of the first ones to reach puberty. Children who are above average in mental test scores tend to be slightly above average in weight and other measures of health. The child who suffers severe emotional stress is likely to fall back in measures of health, growth, and school attainment in the same period.

Though all aspects of growth appear to be related there may still be some that differ from others. Willard Olson saw the value of having some single figure that would indicate the child's true developmental age more accurately than does his chronological. He averaged several ages such as reading, mental, grip, dentition, height, and weight, and called the result the "organismic age." This has come to be recognized as the best single measure of the child's degree of maturity.

The Growing Child Resists Displacement from His Basic Growth Pattern

After a period of illness involving physical, emotional, and mental retardation, most children eventually return to the position in the growth curve which would have been attained had they not been delayed. While this principle holds true in general, there are of course illnesses of such extremity that the child apparently never does catch up.

Conversely, when children undergo some special stimulant to growth, such as intensive reading instruction or vocabulary training, they remain advanced while they are under the unusual pressure but lose their lead, once the special attention is withdrawn. If, however, the special training is needed because of previous poor training, then the improvement may be permanent providing that subsequent teaching is effective.

Growth Patterns Are Unique

Children have unique variations in their rates of growth. The increasing evidence indicating the highly individual nature of growth patterns causes us to question the "constancy of the IQ." It is now well established that the child's IQ at age two is no sure measure of his IQ at age twelve. The IQ's of his parents give a much more reliable indication of the infant's eventual performance than does his early behavior. Once he arrives at school his performance becomes more stable but even here it is subject to sweeping changes. Teachers have reported many children who have made striking changes in their rate of learning without any apparent change in external circumstances.

Sequence of Development Is Dependable and Predictable; Exact Timing Is Not

In the events of physical growth and development and in the appearance of fundamental activities such as walking, running, talking, and use of the hands, the sequence of happenings is dependable, the same for all children. Though the time of occurrence will be early for one child and late for another, all children will crawl before they walk, babble before they utter words with meaning, scribble before they write. All will show a growth spurt before the arrival of puberty. In many events that are not so completely "physical," sequences of development are still quite dependable. The child at play passes from no rules to a stage in which rules are worshipped or exaggerated to a final stage in which rules are regarded with moderation.

Intervening steps of development may sometimes be omitted,

ALL CHILDREN SAME; EACH DIFFERENT

as though a runner passed from first to third base without touching second. It is generally agreed that such omissions are apparent only and that the intermediate stage was present but not noticed by the parent or other observer.

So certain is this sequence of events in motor development that tables of "motor age" have been prepared based on the observation of many children. By matching a young child's typical activities with the corresponding place in the table his motor age may be read. Essentially this is the method used in determining "mental age" and IQ.

HOW TO INTERPRET CHAPTERS 2 THROUGH 7

The reader must constantly bear in mind the limitations of the available research establishing characteristic behaviors at various ages. At all times he must maintain a critical, questioning, tentative frame of mind. Most of the investigations of children have been based on a small group, sometimes as few as twenty-five, rarely more than a few hundred, and typically from one or at the most several different communities. The major exceptions are four recent nation-wide surveys of adolescents. (The three most relevant to this booklet are described by annotations in Appendix IV: 2, 9, 13.)

Some of the investigations of children are based on "problem" children at child guidance or juvenile correction centers. The majority, however, are confined to middle- and upper-class children attending school in urban areas. Children in rural areas and in the lower socio-economic class are missed because of inconvenience for the researcher or because they are not in school.

This bias in selection means that the reader who is studying rural or lower socio-economic level children will have to bear in mind the ways in which they are known to differ from the reported research "average." For example, rural adolescents are likely to have more part-time and summer work than the majority of youth, who are city dwellers. Children in the lower economic classes tend to have a more negative attitude toward school than do other children. This precaution is not needed for the interpretation of the many patterns of behavior which are little affected by social class or rural-urban variation.

Another kind of limitation which applies to a small portion of the research on which this pamphlet is based is that it may be ten or fifteen years old, with nothing more recent available to supplant it. Yet it must be recognized that social behaviors such as dating, reading interests, or part-time work may be changing rapidly. The more obviously physical characteristics are more stable, but even they are slowly changing. Youth today are taller than were their parents at comparable ages, and girls today menstruate at an earlier age than did their mothers.

Most researchers are well aware of the limitations in the selection of their subjects, and their failure to keep studies current. These inadequacies will continue until society is willing to spend more money for finding out about children.

After recognizing the existence of the limitations which have been enumerated, it is reassuring to know that the statements of characteristics in this book represent substantial agreement, however different may have been the researchers, their times and places, and their selection of subjects.

Errors of reporting and interpretation are unavoidable in the various stages from original research to its report in summaries such as the present book. In all research, whether in human behavior or nuclear physics, these errors are inevitable. For these many reasons the reader must maintain the critical, questioning, tentative frame of mind.

The authors would like to think of a reader saying to himself: "This characteristic probably is true for most children of this age, likely it will be true for my child—it's possible that it is wrong—I'll take a fresh look and see if it fits him."

Another limitation, of special significance to the later chapters, is the fact that the older the child, the less the reliance that can be placed on generalizations about typical behavior. As heredity and environment have longer to operate, older children become increasingly dissimilar.

More reliance can be placed on characteristics closely related to physical structure, less can be placed on characteristics highly responsive to environmental variations. Statements about the capacity of children's vision around age five or six are more dependable than generalizations about the skating or swimming skills at the same age. Statements about the time of voice changes for adolescent boys are much more dependable than statements about their vocational aspirations.

The reader should not interpret the statement that a particular behavior is typical in a given age group to imply approval or disapproval by the authors. Obviously little or nothing is to be done to alter biological characteristics, such as the appearance of sex developments. But much could and perhaps ought to be done to improve the situation or climate surrounding the child so as to bring changes in reading interests, part-time work, or group membership. Such judgments are left up to the reader. The characteristics are offered as simple statements of fact.

Yet another misinterpretation is possible. If the parent or teacher regards the statements about typical behaviors as standards or norms for an age and presses the child to "equal" or "surpass" them, this booklet is being misused and the child will suffer. Each child must be allowed to develop at his own rate and in his own way. It is sometimes difficult to draw the line between helping and forcing. But this fact does not relieve the teacher or parent from giving as much help with as little forcing as possible.

ORGANIZATION OF THIS BOOKLET

The remaining six chapters of this handbook contain descriptions of the characteristic behaviors of children at each of six stages from birth to adulthood. The division points of these stages reflect the influence of the research of Herbert Stolz, who studied the growth patterns of boys over their first two decades. He showed that the rate of increase in size took the form indicated in Figure 1 when percentage increase in stem length (approximately the same as sitting height) every six months was plotted against age. The six categories used in this booklet are also labeled in Figure 1.

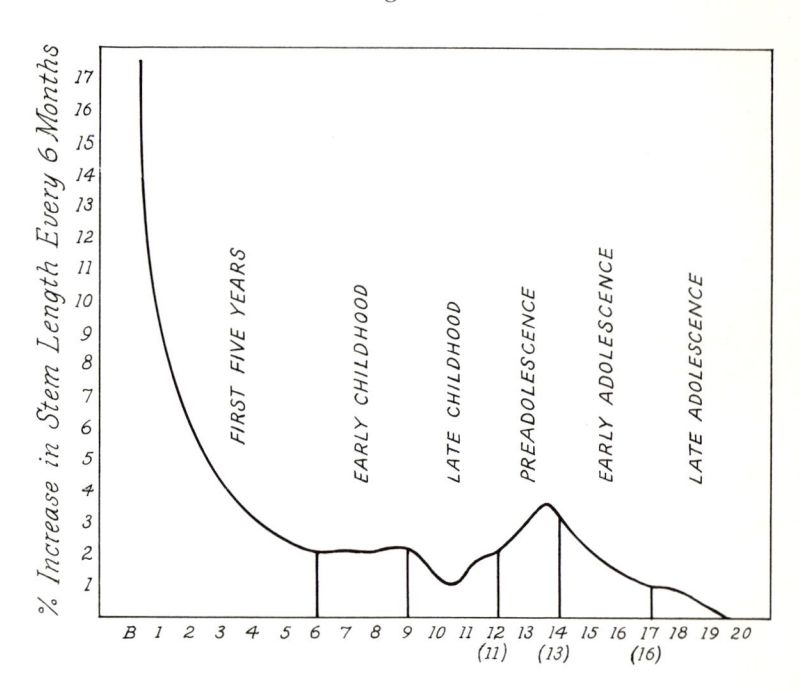

ALL CHILDREN SAME; EACH DIFFERENT

The figures in parentheses in Figure 1 are ages of girls, representing their lead over boys. Depending upon the aspect of maturity which is selected, the lead of girls over boys is variously reported as ranging from one to two years. Arbitrarily the authors have chosen the one-year differential. Also it will be noted that this booklet departs from usual practices by maintaining this differential in defining the end of later childhood, preadolescence, and early adolescence.

A brief overview of the six stages follows:

First Five Years (Chapter 2)

Because this booklet is primarily concerned with school-age children, this section concentrates on behavior characteristics of five-year-olds, with a smaller amount of material on the earlier years. Most children in the first five years progress from the complete dependence of early infancy through the uninhibited twos, the more orderly threes, the vigorous, socially curious fours, and the more co-operative fives.

Early Childhood, Ages 6, 7, and 8 (Chapter 3)

This is a period of steady growth. The entry of children into the first grade is a smooth, pleasant transition in some schools, and an abrupt, painful change in others. The orientation of the child at age six is still toward the parent and the teachers. At eight, it is beginning to be toward his peers, that is, other children of the same age.

Later Childhood, Boys: 9, 10, and 11; Girls: 9 and 10 (Chapter 4)

The rate of growth declines in the latter part of this period. This is a serene stage in most ways. By the end of later childhood the superiority of girls over boys in height becomes apparent.

Preadolescence, Boys: 12 and 13; Girls: 11 and 12 (Chapter 5)

This is the period of most rapid growth. The terminal of preadolescence is sometimes called puberty. Others see puberty as a period of several months or longer covering the most rapid changes in sex characteristics.

Early Adolescence, Boys: 14, 15, and 16; Girls: 13, 14, and 15 (Chapter 6)

Mature sexual capacity and almost mature bodies require these youngsters to make difficult adjustments. They may be expected to behave as adults and then be treated like children.

They are neither. They are absorbed in learning how to relate to their peers, and especially to the opposite sex. The kind of foundation built in the earlier years helps to determine whether adolescence brings severe frustration or satisfying development toward maturity.

Late Adolescence, Boys: 17 through 20; Girls: 16 through 20) (Chapter 7)

They move out on widely separated paths. Some are already carrying the responsibilities of maturity. Others at the end of this period will for various reasons still not be ready for full adulthood.

Within each of the following six chapters, the characteristics are organized under a system of five main headings: physical, emotional, social, mental, and moral and spiritual development. These categories were selected because of convenience and because it was assumed that readers would find them familiar and accustomed. As with any set of categories, they posed some difficult logical problems. Many of the statements might with equal justification have been placed under any of two or three headings. For example, "adolescent girls do a great deal of letter writing," might fall under "mental" or "social." That so many characteristics have been placed in the category of social may be an admission of the tendency of the authors to think of a behavior first in its social terms. The paucity of items under the heading of "moral and spiritual" is a reflection on the inadequacies of available research, not upon the nature of children.

At the conclusion of the main body of the booklet, the reader will find appendixes which offer weights and heights of children, a chronology of developments related to puberty, and lists of books, periodicals, and films supplementing this booklet.

REFERENCES

The following references to be found in the Appendixes were most frequently used in the preparation of Chapter 1. The Roman numerals identify the Appendix and the Arabic the item within it.

III. 4, 7, 9, 10, 13, 19, 20, 22, 25.

IV. 4, 10, 12.

V. 10, 12, 13.

These next references are of special value for the beginning students of growth and development.

III. 5 through 13, 15, 25, 27, 28, 29, 31.

IV. 2, 4, 6, 13.

V. All references in this appendix are easy and useful reading for the beginning student. However, they do not attempt a systematic presentation of the theories underlying growth and development.

VI. All films in this section have been produced under the direction of specialists in child development. They are useful and accurate supplements to any systematic study of the subject.

Those parents with some formal preparation in psychology or an unusual interest in the subject will enjoy any of the references in the appendices. The items below will be of value to those with less specialized education and interests.

III. 6, 9, 10, 12, 15, 27, 28.

IV. 6.

V. All references here are of general interest with the exception of a few devoted to a more intensive consideration of sociological and anthropological contributions. The exceptions are: 9, 10, 11, 12, 13.

IV. Without exception the films are of interest and value to parents.

2

Characteristics of Children in Infancy

first 5 years

BABYHOOD THROUGH THE FIFTH YEAR
(THROUGH KINDERGARTEN)

This chapter includes a brief description of the first four years of life and a more detailed study of the fifth, when most children are in kindergarten. Out of the large amount of evidence available on the preschool child only those items have been selected that make a major contribution to the kindergarten teacher's understanding of her pupils as they first arrive at school.

These are the years when we can identify with most certainty the characteristics of children at each age level. While their behavior already differs widely from one child to another due to a range of acquired characteristics and backgrounds, age mates have much more in common than will be true in later stages.

By kindergarten, girls are almost a year ahead of boys in their growth to maturity. However, the greater comparative size of the male at all developmental stages cancels the girls' lead in height and weight.

These first years have an influence far beyond all others in determining the child's eventual personality. By the time he enters kindergarten he possesses a well-formed picture of himself

in relation to the physical and social worlds around him.
In the first two years the typical child becomes acquainted with his body, learns to walk, begins to talk, begins to reason, and emerges from the complete dependence of babyhood. Around his second birthday he moves into a period of great and active curiosity about his physical environment. With little regard for mother's nerves he opens, pulls down, or pulls apart everything within reach. By his third birthday he has come to terms with his physical environment and mother gets a breathing spell. With his fourth birthday comes a growing interest in the social world around him. He asks countless questions. He loses the comfortable conformity of three. He rebels against parents and quarrels with playmates. Fortunately for the anxious parent this stage terminates around the fifth birthday. He is now much more grown up. He is ready to fit into a group, will accept the teacher's leadership, will stay with one activity for a longer period of time and, in general, is ready for the restrictions and opportunities of kindergarten.

See Appendix I for average weights and heights.

Characteristics in this chapter apply to most one-to five-year-olds. But some of these children, in at least some respects, will be in the six- to eight-year-old stage. The reader is therefore advised to supplement the present chapter by reading the following one. He is also reminded that the material in this book does not enable the layman to make a dependable appraisal of any child as either retarded or gifted. This can be done only by the expert.

PHYSICAL DEVELOPMENT

Growth

1. There is a steady decline from the initial high rate of growth through this period. In the fifth year they gain two to three inches and three to six pounds.

2. By three they have a full set of temporary teeth; at six the first permanent ones arrive.

3. The average child is still somewhat far-sighted by the end of this period. Many authorities warn against close work for these young children.

4. Growth in large-muscle co-ordination is impressive; finger and hand muscles show less development. At two and one-half years these children can thread large beads; at three use a pegboard; at four use blunt-pointed scissors; by five paint with a large brush, but not write. The five-year-olds are likely to upset materials because of still imperfect eye-hand co-ordination. They need plenty of arm, leg, and trunk exercise.

5. By two most infants will go to the toilet when they feel the need; by three most will stay dry all night. However, there is a wide range of "normal" behavior.

6. At two and one-half years they need some help with meals; by four they have considerable independence.

7. By five years handedness is established. Ninety per cent are right-handed.

Activities

8. Once walking and running are mastered children are constantly active. They need lots of room, preferably outside.

Without plenty of large-muscle activity they become restless and irritable. They run, jump, balance, climb, slide, and swing. They ride tricycles.

9. Beginning at two and one-half years they can make rhythmic use of their bodies in a creative way by clapping, galloping, running, and walking on tip-toe to music. At four they are ready for rhythm band and simple singing games with several children.

10. At five they are skillful with wheel toys, ball, ladder, or a bridge of planks. The better co-ordinated can use roller skates and stilts; some girls are able to jump rope in a clumsy fashion.

11. At three they enjoy simple imaginative play. By five they are able to amuse themselves with quiet play using blocks, paints, clay, puzzles, or simple tools.

Health

12. They are susceptible to infectious diseases, alimentary in summer and fall, respiratory in winter and spring.

13. Because of low calcification, bones are not brittle and there are few breaks.

14. At four they require up to twelve hours of sleep per night; by five eleven will do. At four they require at least an hour's afternoon nap; by five a rest period is sufficient.

EMOTIONAL DEVELOPMENT

Growth

1. By the end of the first year they can express many emotions. The method of expressing them varies through the period. At eighteen months they display temper by lying on the ground and kicking their feet. At four years they kick at people. By five they will generally restrain such physical outbursts and use language to express their feelings.

2. In very general terms we can say that the demanding two becomes the peaceful three, the rebellious four, and finally the calm, dependable, serene five. Girls will lead boys by a few months through these stages.

3. Complete dependence on mother and family is the great need through the first year. With this as a foundation the child

CHARACTERISTICS OF CHILDREN IN INFANCY

is ready to begin the long road to independence in the second year. Without this foundation the child may never achieve full independence. A wide variety of experiences in which he develops growing competence is necessary at all stages in developing independence.

Problems: Irritating but Temporary

4. The two-year-old has reached a stage where curiosity about his physical environment can cause problems for the unsuspecting parent. Books are taken from shelves repeatedly, and the contents of drawers are spread all over the room. Life is more pleasant for both parents and children where prized family possessions are out of reach and where interesting and durable objects are close at hand.

5. At two and one-half he enters an "imperial state" where he insists on having his own way. This passes in several months if crises are kept to a minimum by understanding parents.

6. At four, rapid steps are made in exploring the complexities of the social world. One minute the child is playing happily with a friend and the next is fighting ruthlessly. Rebellion is just below the surface much of the time. By trial and error the child works out many personal relationships. He is constantly appraising himself and others.

7. Negativism is at a high point in the second and third years. It grows out of a desire for independence and difficulty in expressing many urges with an inadequate vocabulary. For those children who receive recognition and understanding negativism is not a serious problem.

Problems: Possibly Persistent

8. Frequent regression to the behavior of an earlier stage may be a symptom of frustration. Occasional regression is normal, especially in early infancy.

CHARACTERISTICS OF CHILDREN IN INFANCY

9. Excessive thumb sucking, masturbation, or other anxiety symptoms should receive attention. They will occur when the child is under severe pressure. Too early or severe toilet training, demands that he finish all food served him, or a general expectation of adult-like behavior may all result in symptoms of frustration.

10. After age three persistent behavior problems are not common and should be regarded as possible symptoms of disturbance. Extreme aggression at five would be regarded much more seriously than the same behavior at an earlier age.

SOCIAL DEVELOPMENT

Peers

1. Adults are more important to them than are peers throughout this period. However, their peers do become increasingly important around four. There is some evidence that successful experiences with peers at this stage make it easier to adjust later when the relationship is more complex.

2. At two and one-half they have difficulty getting along with other children. They are likely to push, slap, or hit as a part of exploring the environment. Their world is still largely egocentric. At three they show more desire to play with other

children. Parallel play begins to give way to associative play, even though they will leave the group at will. They begin to understand sharing and taking turns. They find it hard to give up what they want but will accept substitutes. At four their need for companionship is stronger even though the likelihood of fighting is greater. They may run away from home in order to get companionship if there are no children near. At five they can participate in a large group if supervised, but are better with six or even fewer children. They generally take turns, respect other's belongings, and do not hit or snatch.

3. At three they sometimes select a special friend and reject others. They will change friends often. At four they may select a friend from the same sex and reject the opposite. They will boast, talk at length, name call, fight, and tattle. At five friendships are stronger and fighting is less. Language is a substitute for grabbing, crying, and pointing.

4. At five they may become jealous of other children's prestige in games, success in school, and friendships.

5. Five-year-olds like to take care of younger children. They insist on being taken into the activities of other siblings even though they may be a nuisance. They organize small play groups of children their own age and younger.

6. Dramatic play becomes common at two and one-half and reaches a high level of frequency at four. They have vivid imaginations at four and may create imaginary playmates or make a teddy bear or doll a companion.

7. Boys and girls have similar interests through this stage. Both will play with dolls. They are not self-conscious about their bodies. With adult teasing or much evidence of sex antagonism among older children they may become conscious of sex differences at four or five.

Family

8. They are deeply attached to mother throughout this period. Especially when troubled or sick they prefer her attention. Father becomes increasingly important to them as they mature. At all stages, however, they want and profit from his attention.

9. Beginning at two and one-half these children will "help"

CHARACTERISTICS OF CHILDREN IN INFANCY

with dishes and dusting now and then. They need and enjoy the feeling of being in all family activities.

10. At three they are capable of extreme jealousy of a young sibling. They need help in accepting a new baby into the family.

Teachers and Other Adults

11. They seek the approval of adults rather than of peers. They are not embarrassed by a display of affection and are much reassured by an adult's smile.

12. At five they are ready to learn how to adjust to the needs of the group and the need for accepting authority. If they fail to make these adjustments at this stage it is difficult to do so later. Before five there are periods of high resistance to authority.

MENTAL DEVELOPMENT

Ability

1. Their typical speaking vocabulary is 300 words at two years, 1,000 at three, 1,500 at four, and 2,200 at five. The three-year-old speaks in complete sentences. The four-year-old is at his most persistent question-asking stage: "Why?" "How?" He is easily

satisfied with almost any answer. It is more a social event than an intellectual quiz. The questions of the five-year-old are more pointed and less frequent.

2. At two their talking is limited to three-word phrases. They follow simple directions. At three they talk to themselves at length and thus gain valuable language experience. By four they tell tales that involve wild flights of fancy. By five they are more factual.

3. From two years on they imitate those around them in great detail. The manners, speech, and general attitudes of the parents are all reflected in the child.

4. Art begins with what, in the eyes of some adults, may look like "disorderly scribbling." Actually, as much important exploration and learning are taking place here as at any later stage. The need for approval, understanding, and encouragement is as great now as later. Two-year-olds can do finger painting and work with clay. At three they color with crayons and draw simple figures. In the fourth year they do these things with more proficiency and admire their handiwork greatly. At five they can cut and paste, and copy letters and numbers.

CHARACTERISTICS OF CHILDREN IN INFANCY 31

5. At three they can identify common colors. They can distinguish between "one," "two," and "a lot of." By five they know the values of common coins. They understand that saving coins brings a larger aggregate.

6. At two they like to look at pictures. At three they explain pictures to others. At five they may begin to puzzle out the meaning of comic pictures.

Interests

7. At two they feed dolls and take them for rides. They play with little cars. At three they ride tricycles, play with trains, and "play house." At four their play ideas move beyond the home and they are "playing store" or "train." At five they begin roller skating. They play house with props and much organization. They are systematic and like things to be "just so."

8. At two they like to hear rhymes. At three they like to be told a series of stories with the same characters and setting. They also like to have stories repeated, and want nothing changed in the retelling. At four they enjoy longer stories and poetry. At five they like stories of animals that talk. This is the age when they most appreciate having stories told or read to them with opportunities for comments and questions.

MORAL AND SPIRITUAL DEVELOPMENT

1. The child's first and probably most impressive experience with "right" and "wrong" is in toilet training. Unreasonable parental expectations can cause severe problems.

2. As they develop through infancy they are able to make an increasing number of choices and to tolerate increasing restriction.

3. By two they may show apparent feelings of guilt. This behavior, however, is probably imitative of older children or parents. They have matured sufficiently, however, by four or five so that a conscience becomes a factor in their behavior. At five, the mere thought of a forbidden act may cause guilt feelings.

4. At all stages they will tattle freely unless home or school shows strong disapproval.

5. By three they may repeat prayers though with little or

no understanding. At four religion is one of the many things that interests them and they may ask many questions. They believe parents to be all-powerful. At five they see God as being responsible for all the details of life. God and Santa Claus are in much the same category in their eyes. Both are real persons.

REFERENCES

The most useful sources of information on characteristics of the first five years are listed below by reference to the appropriate appendix. Many other sources in the appendixes offer additional help.

III. 11, 15, 19, 24, 27, 28.

IV. 4, 6, 11.

V. 2, 3, 4, 6, 24, 31, 34, 39, 40, 44, 45.

VI. 2, 3, 13, 16, 19, 21.

3

Characteristics of Children in Early Childhood

ages 6, 7, 8

AGES 6, 7, AND 8 (GRADES ONE, TWO, AND THREE)

There is still a good deal of the baby in the six-year-old child. He cannot read or write, he probably does not play out of sight of home, and he looks constantly to mother for assurance and help, even with dressing. He may even call his teacher "mother." In contrast, the eight-year-old is becoming an assured and resolute child. He can explore new worlds through reading, and he plays happily some distance from home. No longer does he regard himself as the pivot of the universe. In fact he now is able to give up some of his own desires in order to fit in with the group, because the group is becoming important to him. He may do things to irritate the teacher in order to gain the approval of his classmates.

This age span is sometimes called a "first adolescence," since the child faces such problems as learning how to assert independence from his parents and how to relate to his peers.

Physical growth is slow and steady. This is the time when the common childhood illnesses are most apt to occur.

See Appendix I for average weights and heights.

Characteristics in this chapter apply to most children in the six-, seven-, and eight-year range. But some of these children, in at least some respects, will be in either the previous or following stages. The reader is therefore advised to supplement the present chapter by reading both those preceding and following. He is again reminded that the material in this book does not enable the layman to make a dependable appraisal of any child as either retarded or gifted. This can be made only by the expert.

PHYSICAL DEVELOPMENT

Growth

1. Annual increases in height and weight are less than in earlier childhood or in preadolescence. Seven-year-olds, for instance, are likely to gain 2 or 3 inches and from 3 to 6 pounds in a year. Especially noticeable are increases in length of legs and arms and in size of hands.

2. The heart is rapidly increasing in size, and the brain has almost attained full adult weight.

3. Front teeth are likely to be missing at the beginning of this period.

4. The eyes of the six-year-old have not yet reached adult size and, because of their shallow shape, are likely to be farsighted. Rubbing of eyes may be observed, and some sixes may not yet be ready for reading. By eight, the eyes are able to accommodate to a considerable amount of reading or other close work.

5. By the end of this age span a dominance of either left or right eye is established.

Health

6. Sleep requirements are around 11 hours at the beginning and 10 hours toward the end of this age span.

7. Though the afternoon nap has probably been given up, daytime rest is needed in the form of periods of quiet activity.

8. Fatigue is common and may not be recognized by the youngster.

9. Poor posture may appear, especially in tall, lanky children.

10. This period is the most likely time for childhood diseases such as measles and mumps. Respiratory diseases are particularly common around age six.

11. During this period these children usually acquire attitudes of modesty and self-consciousness about sex organs and nudity.

Activities

12. These children tend to involve the whole body in physical activities and find it hard to control their motions. They tire easily and frequently need to change to quiet amusements.

13. Although clumsy and crude in the use of their hands early in this period, they enjoy and do quite well at pasting, cutting, painting, drawing, and handling simple tools such as a light hammer or saw.

14. Enjoyable activities include jumping rope, hopscotch, playing with a ball, ring-toss, tiddlywinks, jacks, tag, hiding, marbles, swimming, kite flying, follow-the-leader, rolling a hoop, spinning tops, and riding a bicycle.

15. Because they are eager to try new experiences, their daring and confidence may often exceed their ability and the limits of caution.

16. These children enjoy rhythmic activities including dancing. Girls like to attend dancing classes and may create original dances. If boys shun these activities, the reason is simply the expectations of the culture, not an inborn sex difference.

17. The demand for vigorous outdoor play increases throughout this period. Running, climbing, handsprings, somersaults, roughhousing, and simple trapeze activities are prevalent.

EMOTIONAL DEVELOPMENT

Growth

1. The major emotional needs, to be valued, wanted, and approved, must be satisfied primarily by parents, secondarily by teachers and other adults. During the latter part of this period the peer group begins to offer some satisfaction of these needs.

Problems: Irritating but Temporary

2. Children of this age may still be quite possessive about the affection and attention of parents and teachers and find it hard to share this relationship with brothers and sisters or classmates. This same reluctance to share affection explains why "two is company, three is a crowd" in play groups.

3. If the strong need to succeed is not satisfied in better ways, these youngsters tell tall stories.

4. Most children at this age have episodes of lying, cheating, and stealing. These terms may be unduly harsh, since generally

CHARACTERISTICS IN EARLY CHILDHOOD

these behaviors are only symptoms of tensions in home and school life and not the result of deliberate malice. Often the basis is merely misunderstanding or immaturity.

5. Tensions in school and at home are released by jiggling legs, tapping feet, knocking knees, grimacing, scowling, humming, and chewing hair. Thumb sucking sometimes returns.

6. Common sources of fear are ghosts, witches, burglars, creatures in cellars or attics and, especially for girls, a man under the bed or in the woods. Boys and girls fear the possibility of not being liked by parents or playmates, of death or loss of mother, of being late for school or for the train, and not finishing school work. Television and movies may stimulate fears.

7. Toward the end of this period fears and worries usually decrease, and children may resolve some of their fears by using a flashlight or having someone else precede them in a dark place. Apparently as a means of overcoming a fear, some of them repeatedly expose themselves to a frightening situation.

Problems: Frequently Persistent

8. Though extreme shyness does not suddenly develop, it may not be fully recognized until the child is in school. Severe cases

generally improve when the child is assisted in learning ways of gaining recognition through some kind of achievement or competence.

SOCIAL DEVELOPMENT

Peers

1. First-graders tend to want to please the teacher and may be regarded as teacher-oriented. A year or two later many begin to be peer-oriented and strive to win the attention and approval of their classmates.

2. Early in this period boys and girls may play together, but best friends are likely to be of the same sex. The tendency for the sexes to separate in interests and activities is pronounced at the end of this period. One sex group may then gang up against the other and engage in attacks, retaliations, and verbal onslaughts.

3. Friendships with other children now occupy a large share of time and attention at this age. These relationships are usually brief and quickly shifting and may go through numerous off-and-on cycles. These children like to share secrets with their friends. They enjoy the idea of having a "best friend," and they may also enjoy having an "enemy."

4. Learning to relate to each other as friends seems to require some behavior which to adult eyes may look unfriendly, such as teasing, name-calling, and quarreling. Boys may engage in punching and roughhouse play with complete good will.

5. Though they now are learning to settle more of their differences with words instead of with physical force, these children may use a good deal of physical aggression. Fist fighting is quite common among boys later in this period.

6. Boasting about one's prowess, possessions, or family is a common means of seeking peer approval.

7. A strong need to win, to lead, or to be first is now prominent in most of these children. Like all attitudes, these are learned in the society, not inborn.

8. They still need to be taught to share and reminded to take turns.

9. Attitudes of discrimination against other races and social

classes are ordinarily not characteristic at this age unless these feelings are emphasized in the immediate environment. However, children in this age group may regard youngsters of other play groups or neighborhoods as "out groups."

10. They are learning to assert their own rights, especially concerning property, and they may stand up for the rights of others, too.

11. Gangs and impromptu clubs, generally poorly organized and uncertain as to membership and purpose, first appear late in this period.

12. The "junior" levels of several national youth organizations appear during this age-span. Girls at age seven may join the Brownies or Bluebirds. Boys at six may become Y.M.C.A. Indian Guides.

13. These children are becoming aware of the feelings of their peers and are concerned and sometimes anxious about being liked.

14. They are sensitive to personal criticism and do not know how to accept failure or loss of prestige. But they may be able to accept some criticisms regarding objects they build or create.

15. They may lead or accept leadership in play groups with perhaps as many as seven or eight members.

16. Their fondness for organized games in the latter part of this period is accompanied by a tendency to worship the rules and to be bossy in insisting that others toe the mark.

17. Boys, especially, are proud to be tallest or largest in the group. They feel inferior if they are the smallest.

Family

18. Efforts to assert independence may take the form of refusals to obey or accusations that parents are unfair, bossy, or too strict.

19. They still think their parents know everything and can do everything. These youngsters usually want to be like a parent or possibly a favored teacher, and they imitate adult mannerisms and strive toward adult standards of performance.

20. Parents and teachers are generally accepted as the recognized source of judgments about right and wrong. Peer-group standards are not noticeable until late in this period.

Teachers and Other Adults

21. Wanting to imitate adults and to feel valued, these children voluntarily attempt to help or assume responsibility in home or in school. Many attempts fail or are incomplete.

22. Tattling, which is not uncommon, may be an attempt to attract adult attention or may help the youngster to verify that his standards correspond with those of adults.

23. Self-assertion in the form of roughness, rudeness, and "pushiness" may require adult restraint.

24. Children at this age are highly sensitive to adult criticism and vulnerable to sarcasm, ridicule, or excessive teasing.

25. Late in this period they may begin to experiment with offensive language or unconventional behavior as a means of shocking adults.

MENTAL DEVELOPMENT

Abilities

1. Effective learning must depend mostly on concrete, sensory experiences and hand work, but toward the end of the period more sitting-and-listening and reading become appropriate. These children are interested in specific information, not generalizations.

2. The interests and curiosity of these children are beginning to reach out beyond the home to the community and to the larger world. The starting point, however, is their immediate activities.

3. At first these children have little concept of time, tend to limit their plans to the here and now, and dawdle over assigned tasks. Midway during this age span most can tell time, and eventually they attain good time concepts, as in mealtime, bedtime, the calendar, and the beginning and end of the school year. They have some awareness of the past and of mortality and have a growing curiosity about people of long ago and their way of life.

4. They are apt to interpret stories narrowly, in the light of their personal experience.

5. They tell riddles, attempt to create slap-stick jokes, and enjoy humorous situations and jokes, even when not in picture

form. They may find it pretty hard to enjoy a joke on themselves.

6. Many have a sense of pitch adequate for a fairly accurate reproduction of familiar songs.

7. Introductory musical and rhythm experiences are appropriate at this age. They like to pick out simple melodies on the piano or song bells and enjoy singing games, action songs, and rounds. Most children are not yet equal to practicing by themselves and hence not ready for regular music lessons.

8. They begin to add names and labels to their pictures. Some relationship between their drawings and the object drawn becomes noticeable at the beginning of this period, yet they are more concerned about reproducing what they feel than about realistic proportion and detail. For example, the man may be larger than the house. By the end of the period drawings show keener observation and greater concern with realistic detail and proportion.

9. They are ready to begin learning a foreign language.
10. They can attain some comprehension of the sources, the value, and the uses of money.
11. The age of six and one-half years is thought to be the average time of readiness for reading, for by this time most children have adequate breadth of interest, mental maturity, and eye development.
12. Toward the end of this age-span, children may read independently. Silent reading will be faster than oral. Girls are likely to be faster in learning reading and writing, and boys tend to excel in arithmetic.
13. Early in this age span they may acquire some knowledge of numbers and may enjoy counting to 100. Then they may learn to count by 2's, 5's, and 10's, and, later in the period, to use simple addition and subtraction combinations and fractions of the order of one-half, one-third, and one-quarter.

Interests

14. A favorite activity is dramatic play or make-believe. The influence of television, movies, and story books will be evident.
15. These are the peak years for reading comic books. Children seem to find satisfaction in identifying with the scamp or mischief-maker who nevertheless is a likeable character, or with the super-hero who conquers evil.
16. The attention span becomes adequate for full-length movies toward the end of this age. They usually prefer animal stories and films with singing and dancing.
17. Questions and other evidence of curiosity about sex are frequent.
18. Girls like to play house and dress up. Doll play is at its peak early in the period. Boys like to play cowboys and robbers. Toward the end of the period they store their varied collections in their pockets.
19. Both sexes enjoy checkers, monopoly, dominoes, elementary card games, or other simple table games.
20. Girls like to think of themselves as nurses, teachers, actresses, or mothers. Boys like to imagine they are airplane pilots, locomotive engineers, or soldiers.
21. These children like to pick up and examine toads, insects, and worms, and they enjoy trips to the zoo. They love pets, but

many of the children are not yet responsible enough to provide dependable care.

22. They will want a weekly allowance and will benefit from the experience. Some may manage to save it for a number of weeks. Many will have trouble in keeping it in a safe place or remembering where they left it. They like to learn to shop and can make simple change. The mere act of making a purchase seems to bring considerable satisfaction even if the purchased item turns out to have little use.

23. Occasional chances to earn small sums of money by means of simple tasks at home or at a neighbor's house will contribute to a sense of achievement and independence.

24. These children want to produce well-made objects. They now put such a premium on correctness that they are said to be in the "eraser stage."

MORAL AND SPIRITUAL DEVELOPMENT

1. At first these children think of *good* and *bad* only in terms of specific acts approved or disapproved by parents. Then ideas of good and bad become broader and more general, as in obeying, helping, hurting, and the like. The idea of being fair becomes important, and moral evaluations are eventually made in terms of *right* and *wrong*.

2. Discussing the right and wrong of their own and other children's actions helps to improve the level of their behavior.

3. Increasingly these children want to feel that they have done what is right and approved. Wrong-doing leaves them worried and unhappy, even though they may be reluctant to confess the act.

4. At first they are likely to regard themselves as the center of the universe, but during this age period they establish a truer perspective of their relationship to other people.

5. The sense of responsibility is adequate for trips of some distance to the store, the playground, or the home of friends.

6. If parents do not expect too much consistency these children can help in such tasks as setting the table, washing the dishes, making their beds, and tidying up their rooms. Successfully establishing this latter habit may require a patient campaign continuing far beyond this age period.

7. They are interested in the idea of God, heaven, and angels. Eventually their questions become thoughtful and appropriate and, toward the end of this period, they may begin to be skeptical, at least to the degree of distinguishing between what they feel they know and what has merely been told to them.

8. They enjoy Sunday school, short rituals, and Bible stories.

9. Prayers are important to them, and they may expect immediate, literal answers. They may like to try a simple grace at meals and may wish mother or father to join them in saying bedtime prayers.

10. They can learn to place more emphasis on giving and less on receiving gifts. The "Santa Claus" idea is generally rejected.

11. Their developing sense of responsibility moves through these stages:

a. Questioned or accused of a misbehavior they have committed, they blame others or may blame an inanimate object.

b. They justify their failures: "I was just going to," "I meant to."

c. They may begin to accept blame, apologize, and feel guilty and contrite. At any rate, if they still deny responsibility, they are less likely to try to shift the blame to others, but may seek to be condoned, asking "How could I help it?" or "Could you blame me?"

12. In the early part of this period they assume that they will not die, but later come to realize that death is universal and that it is connected with old age, sickness, and accident. The thought of the death of children and of animals may disturb them, and they are likely to fear the loss of a parent through death. Funerals, burials, and cemeteries may arouse interest and questions. Toward the end of this period they are interested in the question of what happens after death.

REFERENCES

The most useful sources of information on characteristics of early childhood are listed below by reference to the appropriate appendix. Many other sources in the appendixes offer additional help.

III. 10, 15, 16, 19, 24, 27, 28, 29.
IV. 4, 6.
V. 4, 25, 41, 46.
VI. 4.

4

Characteristics of Children in Later Childhood

ages 9 to 11

BOYS: AGES 9, 10, AND 11 (GRADES 4, 5, AND 6)
GIRLS: AGES 9 AND 10 (GRADES 4 AND 5)

Girls move into preadolescence a year or more ahead of boys. For this reason we group girls ages nine and ten with boys ages nine, ten, and eleven in the category "later childhood." The girls maintain their lead through the next seven or eight years.

Later childhood is a period of comparative serenity. It will be several years before these children again adjust to life so smoothly. In a good setting they are eager to learn. They are most interested in the physical world around them. They thoroughly enjoy the school that lets them study science. While the gang is important, they are willing to accept the leadership of the teacher.

Through later childhood the behavior of boys and girls diverges. Boys continue rough-and-tumble activities; girls become more lady-like.

They appear to have so few problems that until recently these were the "forgotten years" in child study. We now recognize the opportunities offered in this stage to help children

CHARACTERISTICS IN LATER CHILDHOOD

develop the skills, understandings, and attitudes that will see them through later complexities as well as current problems.

See Appendix I for average weights and heights.

Characteristics in this chapter apply to most children in the indicated age range. But some of these children, in at least some respects, will be in either the previous or following stages. The reader is therefore advised to supplement the present chapter by reading those both preceding and following. He is again reminded that the material in this book does not enable the layman to make a dependable appraisal of any child as either retarded or gifted. This can be done only by the expert.

PHYSICAL DEVELOPMENT

Growth

1. Growth in height and weight continues steady until the last few months, when there is a sharp decrease.

2. These children require 2400 calories daily, compared with the average adult requirement of 2500 to 3000.

3. Fine muscles begin rapid development through this period and make enjoyable such activities as playing musical instruments, baseball, apparatus work in gym, hammering, and sawing. For many girls these are the last years of interest in such large-muscle activities as running and jumping.

4. Physical co-ordination, by the end of this period, has advanced to the point where the child may write as legibly as his parents. However, there are enough relapses into awkward behavior to make dropping the pencil not uncommon. His deficiencies in co-ordination will also be apparent in organized athletics.

5. The eyes are mature and long reading sessions are possible without strain.

Health

6. These are the most healthy years of their lives. They enjoy a respite between childhood and adult diseases.

7. They may still refuse some foods, especially novel dishes, but this is less a problem than formerly.

8. The good posture of former years is frequently lost. Both

parents and teacher should encourage proper positions in writing and walking.

9. They require 10 to 11 hours sleep. There should be rest periods through the day.

10. Overstimulation is possible, particularly in rigorous, competitive games. According to many authorities the development of the heart has not kept up with that of other organs. Tiring places in games, such as pitcher in baseball, should be rotated frequently.

Activities

11. Boys still enjoy roughhousing, swimming, skating, "cowboys," and all games involving excited running. They now enjoy more highly organized games such as baseball or overnight hikes. The girls are changing from active to more sedate activities, though the former still have much attraction.

12. Some encouragement may be required by parent or teacher to develop physical skills. They are important at this age in establishing the boys with their peer groups.

EMOTIONAL DEVELOPMENT

Growth

1. In general, this is a period of good emotional as well as physical health. These children are primarily concerned with simple, concrete physical problems that can be dealt with readily, such as collecting stamps or making model ships. This period of comparative serenity provides an opportunity to help them develop the self-confidence and understandings that provide a foundation for meeting the greater problems of adolescence.

2. The basic emotional needs continue to be the same—love, belonging, security, success, new experiences, and independence.

3. There is a marked increase in control of the expression of emotions, though there will be some outbursts. "Getting even" becomes more subtle. There is less open expression of love to parents. While these children feel ashamed when they cry they will do so if overtired, angry, or if their feelings are hurt.

4. Girls show their affection by putting their arms around each other; boys by punching.

Problems: Irritating but Temporary

5. Some behavior is irritating to some adults, for example, silly tricks, laughter for no apparent reason, or secret codes. Boys, especially, will try vulgar words, but will discontinue them quickly if treated in a casual manner.

6. Signs of growing independence, such as rebelliousness, disobedience, backtalk, discourtesy, are common. Parents and teachers should recognize them for what they are and not misinterpret them as incipient delinquency. A "man-to-man" talk about good manners and a recognition of their growing independence will generally keep such behavior within acceptable bounds.

7. The demands of the gang may bring its members into conflict with parents. Encouraging the members of the gang to visit in the home may be part of the solution.

Problems: Frequently Persistent

8. Attention should be given to behavior that indicates failure to grow emotionally, such as withdrawal, cruelty, persistent

discouragement, excessive day dreaming, truancy, or depression.

9. Poor physical health may lead to poor mental health. The reverse may happen but is less likely than in later periods.

10. While fears are not as common as before, they do exist and should never be ridiculed. Common fears include the unfamiliar, the teacher, failure, unpopularity, death, and family problems.

11. Poor reading skills can lead to frustration. The reading problem may be either the cause or the result of the emotional problem. Poor instruction, delayed maturity, or low native ability can all retard reading.

SOCIAL DEVELOPMENT

Peers

1. The importance of the peer group increases but the affection, confidence, and recognition of adults continue to be important. Parental domination or overprotection is strongly resented when peers are present.

2. The influence of the peer group on dress, activities, and values is increasing. Those who fail to conform may know the bitterness of rejection. The group disciplines its members with harsh justice, such as using unflattering nicknames.

3. The standards of the peer group will generally prevail over those of the adults. Parents and teachers often work with the total group in order to help some individual in it. In school, good group standards are more effective than adult standards.

4. These children are more likely to accept adult values in relations with other races and social classes. They are ready for insightful discussion and understanding of social relationships. Prejudices can become established at this period.

5. The gang to which the child belongs is characterized by secrecy, passwords and signs, small membership (from three to ten children), rules, changing membership, and strong feelings.

6. Boys and girls do not play together with the ease of former years. There may even be strong antagonism between them. Their clubs are separate; they speak critically of each other. This sex antagonism lasts longer for the boys.

7. Team games become more common at this stage. Success on the team is an important way of obtaining status for many boys. They are loyal to the team. Skillful adult leadership is important.

8. Girls attain status by their manner of dressing. They are more conscious of their appearance than are boys.

Family

9. They continue to enjoy activities with adults and parents but resent domination. Independence is important. Their greater maturity means that there are more activities they and parents can enjoy together.

10. They discuss and evaluate teachers and parents.

11. Their world is moving far beyond the home. However, they still appreciate their positions in the family. They like to be included in making plans and discussing the budget. They will accept home responsibilities, if reminded, provided that they are not out of line with those of their friends. They turn to the family for support in facing their expanding world.

12. Disagreements and fights with brothers and sisters are still common though not serious.

13. There is some tendency in this as in subsequent stages for the popular child to come from the culturally and economically superior home.

14. His curiosity about sex becomes more detailed at this stage. Jokes related to it become common. He is ready for lengthy, analytical discussions with parents. They must frequently correct misinformation obtained from the peer group.

CHARACTERISTICS IN LATER CHILDHOOD

Teachers and Other Adults

15. These children like a "fair" teacher and will accept friendly advice from him. They may show group opposition to the disliked teacher. They may gang up on the "teacher's pet."

16. They tend to be indifferent to good manners but will respond well to class and home discussions about them. The attitude of the gang is important in this as in other affairs.

17. They enjoy both co-operation and limited competition. They find co-operation difficult to learn, competition easy. Adults can set up for these children rigorous competition, which frequently leads to severe emotional disturbances.

18. Hero worship is common. The entertainment world, especially television, provides most of the heroes and heroines.

MENTAL DEVELOPMENT

Ability

1. By grade 5 they use reading as much as direct experience to increase knowledge. By grade 6 they can readily make the discriminations of time and space required for geography and history. Many are able to begin algebra.

2. In rote memory, pitch discrimination, and general neural development they are almost adult. However, their limited experience generally holds performance well below adult levels.

3. This is a period of rapidly increasing ability in abstract thought. They can understand a word such as *pity*, though one like *democracy* has less meaning.

4. They can make plans and modify them for periods covering several weeks.

5. They can evaluate their own activities and productions with insight.

6. Their attention span continues to increase. For subjects such as arithmetic twenty-five minutes would be a good concentration period. They may work on something with variety and immediate interest for hours.

7. There is a great range of reading ability, with some reaching adult levels by eleven years. A few will be several grades retarded.

8. Through this period they develop paragraph skills. They write letters, stories (with many animal characters), and school newspaper items. They need many kinds of opportunities to express themselves both at home and at school.

9. By the end of this period and into preadolescence they may be reading more than at any other time in life. They have mastered the mechanics of reading and it provides them with an avenue into many interests. Later on the many social activities of adolescence will limit reading.

10. Along with the increased reading is a growing vocabulary. By junior high school the typical student uses 7,500 words.

11. New maturity makes creative companionship with parents more possible. Together they may read and discuss books related to social studies and other parts of the school program. These can be satisfying and stimulating experiences for both parents and children.

Interests

12. Their interests are expanding into other parts of the world and into events in the distant past.

13. Interest in imaginative play lessens, though still strong for many. It is replaced by an interest in facts. They want things to be real, true.

14. Science ranks high in their interests. They will experiment to answer questions. They can identify cars and planes. They enjoy field trips to find out how things work.

15. Both boys and girls like books about travel, biography, science, nature, home, and school. Boys do not like books featuring girls, though girls like those with boys. Boys especially like books of adventure, explorations, the wild west, and mysteries.

16. Interest in collections reaches a peak through this period. These children like to organize their collections. They like to compare theirs with others.

17. Sometimes interest in finding how things work and making collections is so keen that it crowds out play.

18. They are interested in adventures in history. Political history has little interest. Life in other cultures and in earlier days has.

CHARACTERISTICS IN LATER CHILDHOOD

19. Their artistic potential begins to be evident. Drama, painting, music, and art may interest them under the direction of a skillful teacher. They get satisfaction out of effective performance in these and other fields.
20. By nine their sense of humor is active and over the next few years may call for much patience on the part of both parents and teachers. The understanding adult will enjoy some of the expression of this new talent.
21. Radio, television, and movies all hold a strong appeal. Good experiences here may increase interest in reading.
22. They may want to earn money for special purposes. They need help in making good use of their allowances.
23. Their interest in vocational selection is increasing. The boys may choose "cowboy" at nine but will be more realistic by eleven. Teaching and nursing rank high with girls through this period.

MORAL AND SPIRITUAL DEVELOPMENT

1. Through this period the child can make substantial growth in his understanding of and feelings toward right and wrong. He

can develop in tolerance, honesty, and justice. Many begin to show deep concern for the welfare of others. Some authorities see this period as "the crucial one for learning the morality of co-operation."

2. There is often a conflict between the morality of the home and that of the gang. In manners, speech, and general behavior the gang will have most influence; in religion, race attitude, and general ideology the home will prevail. The parent or teacher who would influence the behavior of a child of this age should work on the attitudes and behavior of all the gang, especially the leader.

3. The delinquent child comes to the attention of society at this age. He has matured to the point where his anti-social attitudes can result in severe violations of the law. Up to this point his behavior is less likely to attract general attention.

4. These children have an oversimplified sense of justice. Parents and teachers must take it into account in their dealings and may occasionally have to help them understand an apparent injustice.

5. These children may have standards for their work that are higher than their potential and they may acquire feelings of guilt from their failure to measure up. Middle-class parents often contribute to this frustration.

6. They can assume responsibility for their own room and for some chores around the home.

7. Stealing may simply be a sign of immaturity with no significant implications, or it may grow out of inner conflict which needs immediate attention.

8. Lying may similarly be of minor importance. It may be just an immature exercise of the imagination, or it may indicate serious unmet emotional needs.

9. Bullying in the third and fourth grades is fairly common, sometimes by children who were formerly submissive. It is less frequent where the children have opportunities for socially approved vigorous action and for success.

10. Attitude toward death varies greatly, depending upon the attitudes of family and community. The general casual response of earlier years is gone.

11. They accept religious teachings with little question and quote them in discussing behavior.

REFERENCES

The most useful sources of information on characteristics of late childhood are listed below by reference to the appropriate appendix. Many other sources in the appendixes offer additional help.

III. 10, 13, 15, 22, 23, 27, 28.
IV. 4, 6.
V. 4, 6, 25, 41, 46.
VI. 4, 5, 8, 14.

5

Characteristics of Preadolescence

ages 11 to 14

BOYS: AGES 12 AND 13 (GRADES 7 AND 8)
GIRLS: AGES 11 AND 12 (GRADES 6 AND 7)

The girls are more than a year ahead of the boys in most phases of development through this period. For both, this stage covers a quick trip from the comparative serenity of childhood to the challenges and complexities of adolescence. Powerful forces bring about sweeping physical and emotional changes. Almost one-third of the girls will have begun menstruation in their twelfth year. Breasts and hips are more adult than childlike. For the boys, the penis is growing rapidly, shoulders and chest are broader and deeper, and the voice is beginning to change. Preadolescents are dependent on wise adult help if these changes are to take place without undue anxieties. Parental patience is required for the flighty and inconsistent behavior that appears from time to time.

Preadolescence is the introduction to the next developmental stage, adolescence, where children learn to come to terms with a new, challenging, and, at times, difficult way of life.

See Appendix I for average weights and heights. Also see Appendix II for a summary of the early stages of puberty.

Characteristics in this chapter apply to most children in the

CHARACTERISTICS OF PREADOLESCENCE

indicated age range. But some of these children, in at least some respects, will be in either the previous or following stages. The reader is therefore advised to supplement the present chapter by reading those both preceding and following. He is again reminded that the material in this book does not enable the layman to make a dependable appraisal of any child as either retarded or gifted. This can be done only by the expert.

PHYSICAL DEVELOPMENT

Growth

1. The slowdown in growth at the end of later childhood is followed in this stage by rapid acceleration.
2. Appetites may be enormous. Boys need up to 4,000 calories, girls to 3,000.
3. There is great variety in weight and height among these children due to the different ages at which they reach the growth spurt.
4. Bones and ligaments are not yet sufficiently formed to withstand heavy pressure. High pyramid formations can do permanent damage to those supporting the weight.
5. Co-ordination is improving though not at adult levels. The emotional problems of some may lead to co-ordination problems. The girls are more precise in their movements than boys.

Health

6. They continue to enjoy comparative freedom from diseases. However, ears, eyes, and especially teeth, may require medical attention. Minor illnesses of short duration are fairly common. Some of these may be imagined but are very real to the child. Some may begin orthodontic treatment.
7. Some may still be fussy about foods.
8. The deterioration in posture first noted in later childhood continues through this period.
9. For most, at least 9 hours of sleep are required.

Activities

10. Endurance is usually not high, perhaps because of the

rapid growth spurt. They can overtire themselves in exciting competition.

11. For many, this is a period of listlessness. The cause may be physical or emotional.

EMOTIONAL DEVELOPMENT

Growth

1. The comparative serenity of later childhood is left behind and emotions begin to play a more obvious part in their lives. They frequently appear to be unable to control them and lose themselves in anger, fear, or love. There is often no relationship between the importance of the situation and the violence of the reaction.

2. They are beginning to experience rapid swings in mood, completing a cycle from extremes of elation to depression within a few hours.

3. The preadolescent's strong emotions can become an asset in developing positive social attitudes. They have strong positive feelings toward ideals that are presented to them effectively.

4. At no age will a child with unmet emotional needs change his behavior to any extent as a result of logical arguments. This is especially true of preadolescents and adolescents.

CHARACTERISTICS OF PREADOLESCENCE 61

Problems: Irritating but temporary

5. Both boisterous and nervous behavior indicate the preadolescents' strangeness with new feelings. They may become less responsible and less obedient. They may be hostile to the adults most loved.

6. Frustrations may grow out of conflicts between parents and peers, an awareness of lack of social skills, or failure to mature at the same rate as others. The early-maturing girl and the late-maturing boy encounter the greatest difficulties.

7. They are much given to secrecy. They like their own room, complete with "keep out" sign.

8. Anger is very common. It may grow out of feelings of inadequacy in the face of new challenges, fatigue associated with rapid growth, feelings of rejection, or simply general feelings of uncertainty.

9. Fears, too, are common.

10. Other responses to unsuccessful experiences are overeating and overactivity.

Problems: Possibly Persistent

11. Overdependence on parents and constant failure to enjoy the company of others should be reviewed carefully. They may be symptoms of problems that can become increasingly serious.

12. Failure to achieve status and belonging to the peer group may lead to loneliness and self-pity.

13. At this stage those with delinquent tendencies come into conflict with the law. They have the knowledge and physical capacity necessary to commit serious offenses.

SOCIAL DEVELOPMENT

Peers

1. Their status with the peer group has become even more important than in later childhood. Adult approval is correspondingly less important even though they show need of it when it is withheld.

2. They feel a growing compulsion to conform to the dress, language, possessions, and general behavior of the peer group.

3. They may look down upon those who are less mature and be greatly impressed by those who are more so. Hero worship is common.

4. By the end of this stage, for most, the "gang" with its out-of-the-way meeting place is changing into the "crowd" often found talking eagerly around the soda fountain.

CHARACTERISTICS OF PREADOLESCENCE

5. They can be much influenced by the behavior codes of groups like the Scouts or Y.M.C.A. if these groups enjoy prestige among their peers.

6. Teamwork is now readily understood and practiced. They can work together effectively on projects and enjoy games involving detailed organization such as baseball and football.

7. Most friendships continue to be formed within the immediate neighborhood or classroom. For some, common interests will lead to friendships further afield.

8. Both friendships and quarrels are becoming more intense though neither is likely to survive for a long time.

9. Boys, more than girls, choose friends from their own sex and express antagonism toward the other. Where girls have boy friends the boys are generally from the next older age group. Preadolescent boys begin to show an interest in girls by teasing and hiding their possessions. Girls who receive such attention gain status with their peers. By the end of this period both boys and girls want mixed parties.

Family

10. The preadolescent shows his concern for his family by anxiety when any member encounters poor health or any other serious problem. However, he is working hard to achieve independence from them and his efforts in this direction are often misinterpreted by parents.

11. Some children at this stage are very much concerned if they feel that they are failing to measure up to parental expectations. Parents sometimes cause serious problems when they demand a level of performance far beyond the child's ability.

Teachers and Other Adults

12. The unsuspecting adult is often confused in working with these children. The preadolescent's ideas about himself are constantly changing. One day, or even one hour, he is acting the role of an adult and the next he is a child again.

13. He may have reached the point where he looks to some adult, other than a parent, for help in understanding the complexities of life. This adult must respect his independence, make him feel that he is being treated as a peer, and be willing to

listen at length as well as to talk. Such a person frequently has a strong influence on the child. This relationship becomes even more important in adolescence.

14. A crush on the teacher is common, especially the girls for the men teachers. This is a highly sentimental feeling and is much different from the relationship described in the previous point.

15. They expect a high level of skill and maturity in teachers and parents.

16. The uncertainties and insecurities of the preadolescent make it difficult for him to accept criticism.

MENTAL DEVELOPMENT

Ability

1. While brain and other neural developments are almost complete, these children lack the experience to enable them to solve many adult problems.

2. They are still most comfortable working on immediate concrete problems though some are now ready to consider in a more mature manner concepts like *democracy*. History begins to have more meaning and they can relate it to present events.

CHARACTERISTICS OF PREADOLESCENCE

3. They are able to apply a scientific problem-solving approach to increasingly complex problems if placed in an environment that encourages it.

4. Some will be satisfied with manipulating and learning the general characteristics of electric bell circuits, for example. Others will go on to discover the basic laws at work and to apply them in new situations.

5. Charts, maps, and diagrams are now useful means of communication.

6. They are able to use good judgment in handling money. If properly prepared, they can budget their allowance and supplementary income without the supervision of adults.

7. The attention span continues to increase with all activities. The most striking gains are in problem solving activities.

8. Their reading rates may be adult.

Interests

9. Their interests are much influenced by their accelerating physical growth, their increasingly strong emotional reactions, and their awareness of the new roles awaiting them in society. While interest in physical science continues, especially for boys, problems of human relationships become increasingly important.

10. They have a much wider variety of interests now. Individual differences in interests become greater.

11. They respond well to opportunities for creative expression. Writing, dramatizing, and painting all allow them to explore and develop new interests and to turn to their own advantage the emotions they are feeling so strongly.

12. They like expressing their thoughts in diaries, poetry, and letters.

13. Reading and collecting equal or exceed the high rates of later childhood.

14. This is the period of much daydreaming. They pretend that they have famous parents, they have been adopted, or they are orphans. Daydreaming may become frequent enough to interfere with school work. They no longer engage in imaginative play.

15. Girls lose interest in playing with dolls. They become preoccupied with themselves and their appearance. They are more prone to wish for success in adult life than are boys.

16. Home responsibilities are expanded. They can wash the car, wash dishes, and look after younger children. They appreciate an increased voice in planning along with these new responsibilities.

MORAL AND SPIRITUAL DEVELOPMENT

1. A conscience becomes more apparent at this stage. These children exhibit strong feelings about honesty, for example. However, more of them than formerly will steal. This may grow out of their greater need for a wide variety of articles, the greater chances of success in stealing, the greater pressure of the gang, and the general emotional instability characteristic of this stage.

2. Feelings of guilt, based on both real and imagined wrongdoings, become common.

3. Their sense of simple justice remains strong and they are quick to challenge the teacher or parent who violates it. However, with guidance, they can be led to understand the need for meeting the problems of different people in different ways.

4. Some will begin to question the religious teachings of the

CHARACTERISTICS OF PREADOLESCENCE

home. Their feelings will be intense, though changeable. By thirteen, boys are dropping out of church and Sunday school at a rapid rate.

5. Prayer becomes more abstract than at earlier stages.

6. Girls demonstrate superior moral knowledge. Parents spend more time with them talking about proper behavior.

7. Children of this age can assume jobs away from home and see them through.

8. By twelve many children will be able to reject an immediate enjoyment such as television for a long-term satisfaction such as earning money.

9. They are ready to accept the other person's point of view and to live in harmony with those with whom they disagree, if in an environment that values these skills. They are beginning to see the possibilities of co-operative group action.

10. They begin to exhibit more concern for others and are willing to be helpful without any tangible reward.

REFERENCES

The most useful sources of information on characteristics of preadolescence are listed below by reference to the appropriate appendix. Many other sources in the appendixes offer additional help.

III. 6, 12, 15, 24, 27, 28, 31.
IV. 2, 4, 6.
V. 4, 25, 41, 46.
VI. 1, 5, 6, 12, 18.

6

Characteristics of Children in Early Adolescence

ages 13 to 16

GIRLS: AGE 13, 14, AND 15 (GRADES 8, 9, AND 10)
BOYS: AGE 14, 15, AND 16 (GRADES 9, 10, AND 11)

The adolescent, in the midst of a long transition from the dependency of childhood to the independence of maturity, must adjust to an almost new body. The preadolescent growth spurt, now tapering off, leaves him nearly adult in physique and appearance. Sex organs mature, and the secondary sex characteristics become complete. These include deepening of the voice, adult development of the shoulders of boys and of the breasts and hips of girls, and adult distribution of body hair.

Now that the peer group is a dominant force, adults often condemn the extent to which it consumes the time, influences the behavior, and shapes the thinking of adolescents. It is easy to overlook the indispensable contribution of peer group relationships toward breaking away from dependency upon parents, learning to be part of a team, measuring oneself against others, reassuring oneself about his adequacy, in short, learning to be a full fledged member of a society of equals. Like the many adults who bow in slavish adherence to the values and expectations of their own groups, adolescents may need help in building and maintaining their individuality within the framework of group life.

Not all are agreed that the problems of adolescence are more serious than those of other periods in life, but they are difficult and sometimes bewildering. They are increased by the conflict in values that has resulted from the swift social changes occurring since today's parents were adolescents—and were therefore learning the values of that era. The fact that parents find it hard to revise their own standards adds to the likelihood of conflicts about money, entertainment, clothing, the automobile, and boy-girl relationships.

The greater number of adolescents are not "problems." They manage to adjust to their environment—or adjust it—so as to live a life that is, on the whole, happy and satisfying to them and to those who come in contact with them. Surprises and disturbances are common ingredients. The adequacy of their preparation for the future is highly dependent upon adult guidance that is firm and insistent in its emphasis upon responsibility and at the same time confident and generous in offering the widest possible scope for making choices and exercising initiative.

See Appendix I for average weights and heights. Also see Appendix II for a summary of pubertal developments.

Characteristics in this chapter apply to most children in the indicated age range. But some of these children, in at least some respects, will be in either the previous or following stages. The reader is therefore advised to supplement the present chapter by reading those both preceding and following. He is again reminded that the material in this book does not enable the layman to make a dependable appraisal of any child as either gifted or retarded. This can be done only by the expert.

PHYSICAL DEVELOPMENT

Growth

1. Girls around age fourteen and boys around fifteen look more like adults than like children.

2. Contours of the body and face become mature. The facial shape is less round, more tapered or elongated toward the jaw. Muscles of boys become firm and hard. The bow-like curve of the hair line above the forehead of the preadolescent boy is now modified by wedge-shaped indentations on each side.

3. As sexual maturity is attained, growth of the bones is completed.

4. The growth spurts of early maturing children are brief and abrupt in beginning and ending. Later maturing children have a more prolonged spurt, more gradual in beginning and ending.

5. Early maturers of both sexes tend eventually to become relatively broad in the hips, and the boys have narrow shoulders. The late maturers of both sexes eventually become somewhat more slender and long-legged. The boys tend to have broad shoulders.

6. The child who is tall in childhood is likely to have his growth spurt early and will be tall as an adult. Thus the earliness of the spurt is associated with eventual tallness as an adult but can not be said to be the cause of this tallness.

7. According to the results of tests of gymnastic skills, such as walking a rail or shooting baskets, the adolescent does not back-slide into awkwardness or clumsiness. The awkwardness commonly attributed to him is probably due to his self-consciousness and lack of skill in newly attempted activities.

8. Physical co-ordination becomes adequate for highly skilled sports, such as track, volleyball, and tennis. Late maturers may still be handicapped by poor co-ordination.

9. Controlled and graceful movement is possible for those who have had training in activities like swimming and dancing.

Health

10. Though the posture of most youngsters continues to improve, it may still be very poor for some. Slumping may accompany fatigue or be habitual among tall girls if they feel self-conscious about their height.

11. Heavy appetites are the rule. Typical daily requirements are 3200 calories for boys and 2800 for girls, as compared to adult needs of 3000 for men and 2500 for women. Breakfasts are often skimpy because of haste. Girls are concerned about

improving their figures and some make ill-advised attempts to reduce.

12. As much as ten hours of sleep may be desirable, but many will wish to imitate the eight-hour habits of adults. A common practice is to catch up on extra sleep on the week ends.

13. The principal causes of death at this age, in order of frequency, are (1) motor vehicle accidents, (2) other accidents, (3) cancerous growths, (4) tuberculosis, and (5) suicide. The incidence of serious accidents is greater for boys than for girls.

14. The fact that the glandular system has not regained a steady, organized state is thought to account for some of the occurrences of nosebleed, headache, "nervousness," acne, and palpitations.

15. Worry and shame resulting from acne or other skin ailments prevalent during this age are probably more serious than the purely physical results. Medical treatment is often successful in alleviating these disorders.

16. Dental care is one of the most common physical needs.

17. Girls seek advice, read magazine articles, and otherwise concentrate on the subject of beauty care, personal grooming, and clothes.

18. A lack of adequate information about sex causes many boys and girls to be uneasy, overcurious, and misinformed on the subject.

19. Feelings and activity related to sex are now more serious and intense, in contrast to the more casual and sporadic aspects of sexuality in the previous age period.

20. Masturbation is believed to be common among girls and almost universal among boys. While it is now well known that this practice, in itself, is not harmful, it is recognized that excessive indulgence is symptomatic of emotional and social maladjustment and may later be a hindrance to good marital relationships.

21. Boys between sixteen and seventeen, according to Kinsey, are sexually more active than at any other time of life, averaging three "outlet" experiences per week, principally masturbation, plus the possibility of coitus or homosexual contacts.

22. The adolescent, particularly the boy, may boast about

imagined sexual experiences in an attempt to gain status with his peer group.

23. The strong urge to engage in sex activity comes not only from the fact that sexual maturity is now attained but also from desires to satisfy curiosity and to feel assured of adequacy and normality.

24. Irregularities and possibly some pain are almost universal experiences during the first year of menstruation and commonly continue for some time subsequently.

25. Conception is not possible until some time after menstruation begins, possibly as much as four years later. In general the time lag is longer for early- than for late-maturing girls.

26. When pregnancy occurs in adolescence, labor is apt to be shorter and mortality of both mother and child is lower. Emotional problems, especially if the mother is unwed, will likely be acute.

EMOTIONAL DEVELOPMENT
Growth

1. Emotional instability and fluctuations in mood are symptoms of uncertain striving toward adulthood and the see-saw shifting between childish dependence and mature independence. The instability of the glandular system at this time is thought to contribute to these ups-and-downs.

2. By the end of this period the adolescent needs to have an accepting attitude toward his physique and his appearance, which by now are virtually mature. Whether or not they approach his ideal, he cannot expect much more change in them; growing up is nearly completed.

Problems: Irritating but Temporary

3. These are some of the common emotional ingredients of the adolescent years: withdrawing, secretive, uncommunicative; expansive, outgoing, confident, sociable; rebellious, blasé, apathetic, indifferent. Certain of these moods may seem to characterize one adolescent for as long as a year; in another youngster they may appear in brief and recurring cycles.

4. Self-consciousness or anxiety may result from sex develop-

ments. Late-maturing boys may be ashamed to be seen in gymnasium dressing rooms. Girls with large breasts may refuse to be seen engaging in running, jumping, or other vigorous activities. Boys with erections and girls undergoing menstruation may have unjustified fears that these events are visible.

5. The early-maturing boy is likely to enjoy leadership, superiority in athletics, and high status in peer groups. These advantages probably outweigh the low rating he receives from those adults who measure his behavior in terms of his size and appearance rather than in terms of his age.

6. The mere presence of differences such as unusual size of feet or shape of ears or nose is often a source of worry. Worry about size continues to be especially acute among small, late-developing boys and large or early-developing girls.

7. Girls worry about popularity, appearance, and social skills. Boys worry about being acceptable to girls. Examinations, achievement in school, and getting along with parents and family are sources of concern for both sexes. For the girls, if not for both sexes, these years may be the most stressful period of the teens.

8. The problem of how far to go in necking and petting may cause considerable inner turmoil.

Problems: Possibly Persistent

9. Especially for girls it is true that not having dates may bring deeper emotional wounds than most adults realize. A more serious problem is that of the adolescent who feels that he is not wanted as a friend in relationships with either the same or opposite sex.

10. If sex is a matter of ignorance, fear, and shame, the teen years will be disturbed and will not prepare for a happy marriage or wholesome family life.

SOCIAL DEVELOPMENT

Peers

1. Friendships now depend less on sameness of grade, or age, or neighborhood than was true in preadolescence. Similarity of physical maturity, abilities, interests, and socio-economic status now becomes more important.

CHARACTERISTICS IN EARLY ADOLESCENCE 75

2. At the same time, the basis of many of the friendships in this period is still an easy, amiable companionship which offers the opportunity to do things together with a minimum of conflict. But a sensitive understanding of the feelings of other persons and responsiveness to their needs are developing in these years, especially among girls. They are ahead of boys not only because our culture encourages these qualities in females but also because many social characteristics seem to keep pace with physical maturity.

3. Boys are more likely to have a wide circle of friends, on a more casual basis. Girls tend to have a smaller but more intimate number of friends. Throughout the teen years they tend to have a closer bond with girl friends than with boy friends.

4. Because of striving and competition accompanying their dating and same-sex friendships, some girls may feel unsure or uneasy about the extent to which they can trust girl friends.

5. Given favorable circumstances, many of the friendships begun in this period may endure for life.

6. Pressures to conform to the peer group may be greater for girls than for boys.

7. Peer pressures maintain fads and oddities in dress, both as to the garments preferred and how they are worn. Toward the end of this period, adult standards of neatness and grooming are pretty well established, at least for dress-up occasions. Many indications at the time of writing this booklet point to a recent shift toward more care and neatness. If true, this development

may serve as a reminder of the possibility of quick changes in any of the reported social behavior characteristics of youth.

8. Soda fountains, drive-ins, and other eating places are among the favorite places where the "crowd," the "gang," or the "bunch" gets together.

9. Members of this age group have an increased interest in and need for skills in participating in group activities, such as discussion, parliamentary procedures, and the mechanics of organizing and operating clubs.

10. In comparison with the typical youth organizations which enlist younger ages, the groups which are likely to attract young people at the end of this age period are those which emphasize social relations with the same or both sexes rather than activities emphasizing the physical environment, such as crafts, hobbies, excursions, and camping. At the same time, the needs of youth in the middle teens are so varied as to call for a wide variety of available clubs and organizations, each specializing in an adult-like activity, such as farming, journalism, debate, working with automobiles, or self-government.

11. The extent of membership of these youths in formal organizations is roughly as follows: national youth organizations, such as scouts, rural-life groups, and the Y.M.C.A. and Y.W.C.A.—about one-half of each sex; school organizations—about one-half of the girls and one-third of the boys; church organizations—about one-half of the girls and one-third of the boys. About a fourth of the girls and a third of the boys belong to no organization. At age fourteen, coinciding with entry into the ninth grade, membership ceases in the Campfire Girls, decreases in the Girl Scouts, and sharply increases in school clubs.

12. Parallel with their accelerated physical development, girls, as compared to boys of the same age, are more advanced or forward in seeking attention of the opposite sex and taking initiative in dancing and parties.

13. Some of the boys and the immature girls will be timid in their relationships with the opposite sex.

14. Some boys and a larger number of girls pass through an intense emotional attachment to a considerably older youth or an adult. The relationship may involve close companionship when between two of the same sex, but is likely to be a

situation of "worship from afar" when between opposite sexes.

15. In most communities, lack of at least a minimum of competence in dancing substantially handicaps participation in coeducational social activities.

16. Progressive stages in boy-girl relationships are mixing with a group at a no-date social gathering, double dating, single dating, and going steady. Many, however, depart from this sequence.

17. The proportion of girls who date at age thirteen is small, but by fourteen, commonly the year for entering the ninth grade, the number increases to more than half.

18. By fourteen, boys date almost as frequently as girls. It is not that boys now equal girls in interest in this experience, but that dating may be more or less demanded by the social situation. It is the thing to do.

19. By the end of this period, two events a week held on the week end is the common pattern for those who date.

20. About one-tenth of the girls of this age group go steady. The duration of such a relationship is likely to be brief, perhaps only a few weeks. Frequent reshuffling occurs. Even though a transfer of a sweater, pin, or other symbol is common, the boy or the girl, and more likely both, may anticipate changing partners after a short time.

21. About half of the girls oppose the idea of going steady, and most who approve do so only with the stipulation that the individuals are mature and have had an opportunity to know a variety of persons of the opposite sex. Boys may admit that their going steady is just a fad, or complain if they feel that a girl is monopolizing their attention.

22. According to popular impression, dating and going steady are both earlier and more prevalent than indicated by the most recent and best available survey data. Possibly both sources are erroneous to some degree. Changes are probably occurring, perhaps fast-moving, and possibly in the direction of increase. Regional differences are undoubtedly large.

Family

23. The adolescent needs from his parents an ever-increasing area of freedom to make his own decisions, coupled with an

equally increasing share of responsibility for the consequences of these decisions. Yet at the same time he needs parental security and support in this confusing and complex transition from childhood to adulthood.

24. Though the attitude may be well concealed from parents, most boys and girls of this age feel dependent upon parental rules and regulations. In spite of the protests which may accompany adolescent efforts toward independence, most youths are likely to regard some degree of limitation by parents as needful and beneficial in matters where young people are not yet ready for complete self-management.

25. Critical attitudes toward parents, disapproval of their sense of humor, and arguments with them are common symptoms of the adolescent striving for independence.

26. Girls, especially, want their home to be attractive to friends. They may be very critical about the house and its furnishings and may seem to want perfection.

27. The most common subjects of conflict between parents and members of this age group include homework, chores, getting along with brothers and sisters, use of the family car, dating, clothes, and choice of friends. Conflict involving the last three items is especially prevalent between the girl and her parents.

28. Preoccupied with peer relationships and his growing world outside the home, the early adolescent may seem "far away" even when the parent who tries to open a discussion or ask questions is sympathetic and does not demand too much.

29. If his capacity for fairness and objectivity has been developed by participation in family councils or family decision-making, the early adolescent can be sufficiently flexible to appreciate the needs and views of his parents. In such councils he can contribute effectively to deciding about use of money, vacations, household tasks, and other everyday affairs.

30. Sexually delinquent behavior, especially that of the girl, is likely to be the outgrowth of a poor parental relationship, characterized by a feeling of rejection, hostility, or unsatisfied emotional needs.

Teachers and Other Adults

31. A teacher or an older friend or relative may be the object of admiration approaching hero worship. Counsel and advice from such a source is likely to be more impressive to the adolescent than that from his parents.

32. Considering the remarkably small percentage of teen-agers who by any reasonable definition can be called juvenile delinquents, adolescents are understandably sensitive and resentful if adults indicate a stereotyped or prejudiced view about the behavior of youth. Even the use by the adult of such terms as *teen-ager* or *adolescent* may, in certain contexts, be interpreted as implying an unjustified condemnation of the whole group.

33. Adolescents easily match the enthusiasm of effective and understanding teachers or other adult leaders. When these youngsters seem blasé and apathetic the answer is to be found in the leadership and in the environment, not in the basic nature of the adolescent.

34. Adolescents find their greatest satisfaction and pride in doing an adult job, giving aid, or in some other way filling an adult-like role.

MENTAL DEVELOPMENT

Abilities

1. The brain is now virtually complete in growth and development by the end of this period. If any abstract and complex ideas and relationships are "over his head," the reason is his lack of experience, not lack of capacity.

2. With reasonable opportunity and help in obtaining background information, these young people are eager to take part in discussions about such topics as news events, politics, world affairs, and social issues.

3. They want and have the capacity to plan and organize their own recreational, athletic, and organizational activities. They need adult guidance in the form of the consultant or adviser in the background, not in the form of the decision-maker on or behind the throne.

4. Toward the end of this age span their highly active sense of humor may become sufficiently mature to be enjoyable to adults.

Interests

5. A ranking of broad types of leisure activities for boys, according to the number reporting participation, places team sports first. Closely following are both formal and informal social activities, the latter including movies, radio, television, and records. Also prevalent are outdoor activities, including camping, hiking, fishing, boating, hunting, and winter sports. Hobbies and individual sports are next. Whether or not they are widely available, swimming, hunting, and working on cars or motorcycles are specific leisure activities which are highly preferred.

6. Among girls the broad classification of formal social activities is both first in preference and reportedly engaged in by the largest number. About as many take part in team sports and in informal social activities. This latter classification includes the mass media of entertainment, as mentioned in the previous paragraph, and also telephoning to friends.

7. Continuing the list of girls' leisure activities in terms of number participating, the next broad groups are individual sports, outdoor activities, and creative pursuits such as music

CHARACTERISTICS IN EARLY ADOLESCENCE 81

and the arts and crafts. Except for swimming, which continues as favorite among girls throughout the teens, participation in sports, outdoor activities, and creative pursuits declines as social activities receive more time. To the extent that sports continue, the motivation tends to be more social than athletic.

8. Early adolescents tend to devote less time to movies and television than do youngsters in the previous age group.

9. Girls may do considerable letter writing.

10. Boys and girls of this age now read more about special subjects according to individual interests and are likely to read a great deal in magazines. Boys especially may read extensively on technical subjects and are likely to enjoy adventure stories. Girls tend to prefer romantic fiction. Both sexes are reading fewer animal stories and comics.

11. However confused and uncertain they may be, many are now giving some thought to future decisions about vocation, college, and marriage.

12. Girls are thinking more about the prospect of a period of employment and independence after completion of their education than about eventual marriage and rearing a family. Further, they tend to think of education primarily as a means of reaching this goal.

13. About 2 out of 3 girls plan to enter nursing, teaching, or secretarial work, each of these jobs representing the three preferred groupings, namely, service to individuals, service to groups, and traditional white-collar or clerical. They tend to select a vocation which will harmonize the requirement of personal achievement with the conflicting demands of family

rearing. They rarely select such a vocation as science, medicine, the theater, or any other goal which would demand prolonged preparation and would otherwise be incompatible with marriage and motherhood.

14. They tend to choose vocations which enable meeting and working with nice people, including potential husbands. They want interesting and pleasant activity and opportunities to leave the home town.

15. Boys tend to select vocations in terms of the skill or content of the work itself and are more interested in the prospect of leadership, prestige, high pay, and being one's own boss.

16. About a third to a half of the boys say they want to enter one of the professions, most frequently engineering. Sales and other white-collar jobs and mechanic or repairman are frequently named.

17. It may be anticipated that choices of both boys and girls will reflect the recent increased attention and prestige related to scientific and technical vocations.

18. Many adolescents will admit that their vocational expectations are more down-to-earth than their preferences. Even so, they tend to overestimate both their abilities and the opportunities to enter the professions. This discrepancy, however, may decrease as automation demands an increase in the proportion of American workers who are trained in technical specialties.

19. Part-time work is now important for numerous reasons, including the amount of time it requires of the early adolescents and the contribution it makes to their financial resources and their prestige. Especially when they hold down a job outside their home, these part-time workers gain an important sense of accomplishment and adequacy. Hence work experience is needed by all, including those who may receive ample spending money from their parents.

20. About two-thirds of the girls of this age earn money during the school year, principally by means of baby sitting and other household help. The comparable number of boys is smaller. Paper routes and bag boy at the grocery store are among the most common jobs.

21. The kinds of part-time work available to girls are more likely to be away from home and offer the further advantage of

a closer identification with and preparation for womanhood. Though boys may have a wider variety of jobs available, more of their work is likely to be at home and to be "boys' work," not identified with an adult role.

MORAL AND SPIRITUAL DEVELOPMENT

1. Many early adolescents mention a parent or other adult relative as the person they most admire or would like to emulate. This choice sometimes reflects sheer lack of contact or experience outside the family. An indication of maturity is the decreasing tendency to name an obvious hero or a glamorous person and the increasing tendency to offer a composite of characteristics of several persons.

2. Though they may ask for more than they can handle, early adolescents need a constantly increasing share of responsibility.

3. They are anticipating adulthood by making more of their own decisions about right and wrong, rather than simply copying the standards of their parents.

4. Girls conform more to parental standards of behavior than do boys. Behavior of either sex which conforms to peer group standards rather than to those of parents is likely to be accompanied by feelings of guilt.

5. Cheating in school work is not uncommon, particularly when students of poor ability are pressed to get good grades.

6. Girls, especially, are concerned about maintaining a good moral reputation, in terms of intimacies with the opposite sex, and tend to reject a girl who does not meet their standards.

7. Except for the minority of adolescents who belong to fundamentalist sects, a conversion or religious awakening, if it occurs, is gradual rather than sudden and dramatic.

8. About half of the members of this age group attend church regularly.

REFERENCES

The most useful sources of information on characteristics of early adolescence are listed by reference to the appropriate appendix. Many other sources in the appendixes offer additional help.

III. 2, 12, 14, 17, 18, 19, 21, 24, 31.
IV. 1, 2, 4, 5, 6, 9, 13, (Items 12, and 17 through 21, though important sources, will be less useful for the general reader.)
V. 26, 38, 42, 47.
VI. 1, 6, 12, 15, 17, 18.

7

Late Adolescence

ages 16 to 20

BOYS: AGE 17 THROUGH 20 (GRADES 12 THROUGH 15)
GIRLS: AGE 16 THROUGH 20 (GRADES 11 THROUGH 15)

As youth approach adulthood, there are few dependable generalizations that can be made about their characteristics. Native differences in capacity are now magnified by nearly two decades of environmental differences as to family climates, socio-economic and ethnic backgrounds, localities, school systems, majors in high school, and opportunities for higher education. Consequently there is an enormous range in interests, goals, activities, and achievements.

A few are married and may already have children, some are launched in their life work, and some of the boys are in military service. Because of the draft and especially because of the demands of specialized higher education, many must postpone marriage and financial independence until some time in the middle twenties.

These young people vary widely in degree of independence and responsibility. A young woman may now be a wife and the mother of children. A young man in wartime might be responsible for the operation of a costly airplane and the lives of his comrades. On the other hand there are college students who still depend on mother to choose their clothes and to remind them to do their homework.

Most of these youth are still striving for a sense of adequacy in their everyday social relationships. They are no longer so dominated by the activities of the peer group and are more independent of it in making decisions and setting standards. Extensive dating and going steady are absorbing activities which lead to the selection of a mate and marriage.

See Appendix I for average weights and heights.

Characteristics in this chapter apply to most youth in the indicated age range. But some of them, in at least some respects, will be in either the previous or following stages. The reader is therefore advised to supplement the present chapter by reading the preceding one.

Because of the brevity of this chapter, some subheadings previously used are now omitted.

PHYSICAL DEVELOPMENT

1. During this period, first girls and then boys attain mature height and weight. Most are now at their lifetime peak in physical co-ordination.

2. For the first time since later childhood, boys and girls of the same age are now in most respects at the same level of physical maturity.

3. The relative amount of participation increases in individual sports and decreases in team games. Boys who remain active in sports are now more likely to specialize in one or two activities and give up others. Both sexes spend more time as spectators.

EMOTIONAL DEVELOPMENT

1. Feelings of confusion and bewilderment are common as youth approach the crossroads of decisions about marriage, vocation, college, and the draft.

2. Even well-endowed college youth have more feelings of inferiority and inadequacy than might be expected. Whether or not such feelings have any objective justification, recognition of them is essential to understanding these youth.

SOCIAL DEVELOPMENT

1. An indication of the increasing prevalence of boy-girl relationships is that by this age, only 1 girl in 10 does not date. The large mixed group or "crowd" of the early adolescent period now is replaced by foursomes and the more intimate twosomes which may be a prelude to courtships.

2. Generally speaking, dating now is characterized by more stability, trust, and depth of feeling and understanding. Some dating, however, continues to be merely a casual means of entertainment, and sometimes is primarily a means of gaining status. It does not necessarily imply courtship as it did in an earlier generation.

3. Numerous experiences of falling in and out of love are likely to help provide the perspective needed for choosing a husband or wife.

4. At this age, going steady is more likely to be a prologue to engagement, involving deeper emotional commitments and a stronger expectation of continuance than was true for going

steady in early adolescence. Even so, the steady relationship for some youth in later as well as in early adolescence may be primarily a matter of "date insurance" or convenience. Marriage may still be only a distant expectation.

5. The proportion of boys and girls who go steady is increasing year by year. Yet there is now more awareness of the disadvantages of the steady state for individuals who are not approaching engagement.

6. For young people who proceed directly from high school to work or marriage, the first few years away from the social network of the school are likely to be lonely and rootless until such time as they establish new relationships in the community.

7. The desire to be financially independent of parents sometimes leads to acquiring jobs that are blind alleys or that interfere unduly with educational activities.

8. Though they want to make their own way independently, these youth still put a premium on good relationships with their parents. A fresh or revived sense of respect for and enjoyment of parents now may develop.

9. Symbols or indicators of various degrees of independence are earning enough for clothes and personal expenses, selecting clothes, determining frequency of going out or hour of return, going to work, driving and owning a car, living away from home, setting up a separate place of abode, taking a full-time job, getting married, and voting.

10. Conflicts with parents now focus more on ideas rather than merely on behaviors.

MENTAL DEVELOPMENT

1. Young people by the end of this period have reached the peak of their mental capacity. This does not mean that the eighteen-year-old, lacking algebra can learn calculus, but that, with adequate background and preparatory training, his capacity to learn it is now as high as it ever will be.

2. There is now a good deal of stability of vocational choices, no longer the frequent shifting characteristic of early adolescents. Changes are still possible, and some youth will move from one niche to another even as late as the twenties or after finishing college.

LATE ADOLESCENCE

3. Appraisal of their abilities continues to be one of their major concerns. They are somewhat more realistic in recognizing their limitations, now that vocational entry draws nearer. But many choices are influenced little by objective knowledge of self and influenced much by the status aspirations of parents or the prestige level which our society attaches to various vocations. A considerable number of these youth have made no vocational choice, and of those who have, many are uninformed about the nature of the work or the necessary training and preparation leading to it.

4. Among girls, anticipations of marriage and family increase but still are secondary to the attention focussed on eventual entry into a period of employment following completion of their education.

5. In the vocational choices of girls, idealistic motives of service decline somewhat. Fewer girls choose nursing, more select secretarial work. These vocations and teaching still constitute the three most popular choices.

6. Consistent with the lesser emphasis males place on social status, boys are somewhat more willing to accept the prospect of a "blue-collar" vocation for themselves than are girls for a future husband.

7. More girls now do work outside the home, especially food service, clerical, and other office work.

8. Many of these youth are under time pressure and have

little flexibility to accommodate new activities. School work has increased, dating is active, part-time work is common and more likely to be on a fixed schedule.

MORAL AND SPIRITUAL DEVELOPMENT

1. Many of these youth are dissatisfied with the church and tend to turn away from it, because it fails to meet their needs.

2. If they are now exercising some independence in working out their own standards of behavior and solutions to ethical problems, conflict with parental preferences will probably ensue.

3. These youth, and especially those who go to college, have more questions and increasing skepticism about the religious as well as the political and economic value systems of their parents. Yet the large majority do not depart fundamentally from the parental choices and affiliations of church, political party, or economic philosophy.

REFERENCES

The list of the most useful sources of information on characteristics of late adolescence is identical with that at the end of Chapter 6, except for the exclusion of IV. 13; and VI. 1, 15, 18.

Appendixes

Appendix I

*PERCENTILES FOR WEIGHT AND HEIGHT OF AMERICAN CHILDREN

How To Use Appendix I

Suppose, for example, the reader wishes to know the average weight of five-year-old girls. First find the heading 5 *yr*. Read to the right for girls (for boys, read to the left). The table indicates that the 50th percentile, that is, the average weight for girls at this age, is 40.5 pounds. The figure 34.8 pounds, located immediately to the left, in the column headed *10*, means that the *lightest 10 per cent of five-year-old girls* weigh less than 34.8 pounds. Correspondingly, the entry of 49.2 in the extreme right hand column, headed *90*, means that the *heaviest 10 per cent of girls* at this age weight 49.2 pounds *or more*. (In other words, 90 per cent of all girls at this age weigh *less* than 49.2 pounds.)

An approximation of the data for the odd years not covered by this table, namely 11, 13, 15, and 17, may be found by calculating the figures intermediate to those given for the adjacent even years.

Percentiles, Boys			Age Measurement	Percentiles, Girls		
10	50	90		10	50	90
			Birth			
6.3	7.5	9.1	Weight, lb.	6.2	7.4	8.6
18.9	19.9	21.0	Length, in.	18.8	19.8	20.4
			3 mo.			
11.1	12.6	14.5	Weight, lb.	10.7	12.4	14.0
22.8	23.8	24.7	Height, in.	22.4	23.4	24.3
			6 mo.			
14.8	16.7	19.2	Weight, lb.	14.1	16.0	18.6
25.2	26.1	27.3	Height, in.	24.6	25.7	26.7
			1 yr.			
19.6	22.2	25.4	Weight, lb.	18.4	21.5	24.8
28.5	29.6	30.7	Height, in.	27.8	29.2	30.2

*From Ernest H. Watson and George H. Lowrey, *Growth and Development of Children* (Chicago, The Yearbook Publishers, revised edition, 1954), pp. 43-44. By permission of the authors and the publishers.

APPENDIX I

Percentiles, Boys			Age Measurement	Percentiles, Girls		
10	50	90		10	50	90
			2 yr.			
24.7	27.7	31.9	Weight, lb.	23.5	27.1	31.7
33.1	34.4	35.9	Height, in.	32.3	34.1	35.8
			3 yr.			
28.7	32.2	36.8	Weight, lb.	27.6	31.8	37.4
36.3	37.9	39.6	Height, in.	35.6	37.7	39.8
			4 yr.			
32.1	36.4	41.4	Weight, lb.	31.2	36.2	43.5
39.1	40.7	42.7	Height, in.	38.4	40.6	43.1
			5 yr.			
35.5	40.5	46.7	Weight, lb.	34.8	40.5	49.2
40.8	42.8	45.2	Height, in.	40.5	42.9	45.4
			6 yr.			
40.9	48.3	56.4	Weight, lb.	39.6	46.5	54.2
43.8	46.3	48.6	Height, in.	43.5	45.6	48.1
			7 yr.			
45.8	54.1	64.4	Weight, lb.	44.5	52.2	61.2
46.0	48.9	51.4	Height, in.	46.0	48.1	50.7
			8 yr.			
51.2	60.1	73.0	Weight, lb.	48.6	58.1	69.9
48.5	51.2	54.0	Height, in.	48.1	50.4	53.0
			9 yr.			
56.3	66.0	81.0	Weight, lb.	52.6	63.8	79.1
50.5	53.3	56.1	Height, in.	50.0	52.3	55.3
			10 yr.			
61.1	71.9	89.9	Weight, lb.	57.1	70.3	89.7
52.3	55.2	58.1	Height, in.	51.8	54.6	57.5
			12 yr.			
72.0	84.4	109.6	Weight, lb.	69.5	87.6	111.5
56.1	58.9	62.2	Height, in.	56.1	59.6	63.2
			14 yr.			
87.2	107.6	136.9	Weight, lb.	91.0	108.4	133.3
59.9	64.0	67.9	Height, in.	60.2	62.8	65.7
			16 yr.			
111.0	129.7	157.3	Weight, lb.	100.9	117.0	141.1
64.1	67.8	70.7	Height, in.	61.5	63.9	66.5
			18 yr.			
120.0	139.0	169.0	Weight, lb.	103.5	119.9	144.5
65.5	68.7	71.8	Height, in.	61.5	64.0	66.7

Appendix II

CHRONOLOGY OF PUBERTAL DEVELOPMENTS IN HEIGHT, WEIGHT, AND SEX CHARACTERISTICS

1. All statements in this sequence are to be understood as applying to boys or girls in the United States *on the average*.
2. Where data are available, the month of occurrence of an event is shown in parentheses after the statement to which it applies. The reader is reminded that the sequence of events is more dependably established than the average age of occurrence.

GIRLS	BOYS
AGE 10 (Fifth Grade)	
Hips begin to widen during age 8 to 10 *Menstruation* begins before age 11 in about three out of 100 girls *Breast* development may begin as early as age 10 for early maturers	
AGE 11 (Sixth Grade)	
During this year girls become taller than boys.	
Preadolescence *Breasts* begin to bud (11-1) *Pubic hair* appears (11-4) *Height:* maximum gain period begins (11-12)	*Testes:* accelerated development begins
AGE 12 (Seventh Grade)	
Girls are taller and heavier than boys.	
Pubic hair is slightly curled (12-1) *Height:* peak of maximum gain period (12-6) *Weight:* peak of maximum gain period coincides with or closely follows that of height *Pubic hair* is moderately curled (12-10)	*Preadolescence* *Height:* maximum gain period begins, and, at about the same time, accelerated development of penis begins *Fat:* for half or more boys, fat is conspicuous around nipples and over abdomen, hips, and thighs

APPENDIX II

GIRLS	BOYS
AGE 13 (Eighth Grade)	
Girls are taller and heavier than boys.	
Early Adolescence *Menstruation* begins (13-2) *Pubic hair* is well established *Hair under arms* appears after first menstruation	*Pubic hair* appears (13-5) (Girls at 11-4) *Voice* change begins *Ejaculation* of semen begins, and, at about the same time, *hair under the arms,* with perspiration odor (13-7)
AGE 14 (Ninth Grade)	
Girls are shorter but heavier than boys.	
Breasts are maturely developed (14-1) *Pubic hair* is maturely developed (14-2)	*Early Adolescence* *Height:* peak of maximum period (Girls at 12-6)
AGE 15 (Tenth Grade)	
Girls are shorter but heavier than boys.	
AGE 16 (Eleventh Grade)	
Girls are shorter and lighter than boys.	
Late Adolescence *Menstruation:* About three out of 100 menstruate first at age 16 or later	*Shaving* becomes necessary between 15 and 17 *Voice changes* are completed between 16 and 18
AGE 17 (Twelfth Grade)	
	Late Adolescence
AGE 18 (Thirteenth Grade)	
Mature height is now attained.	

Appendix III

TEXTBOOKS ON CHILD DEVELOPMENT

The following texts have all made contributions to the conclusions of this book. Those with detailed reports on research and with their own lists of characteristics have been of particular use.

The several books of readings have been used in classes much as regular textbooks and therefore have been included in this section.

1. ALMY, Millie, *Child Development* (New York, Henry Holt and Company, Inc., 1955).
   Relates research findings and principles of development to the life histories of six young people from birth to eighteen.
2. AUSUBEL, David P., *Theory and Problems of Adolescent Development* (New York, Grune and Stratton, Inc., 1954).
   Thoroughgoing and carefully written. Rewarding for the advanced student but too difficult for most laymen. More space devoted to organization and interpretation of research findings than to reporting research itself.
3. BALDWIN, Alfred L., *Behavior and Development in Childhood* (New York, The Dryden Press, 1955).
   More suitable for the advanced student. A careful distinction between the concepts of behavior and development is basic to the organization of the book.
4. BARKER, R. G., KOUNIN, J. S., and WRIGHT, Herbert F., editors, *Child Behavior and Development* (New York and London, McGraw-Hill Book Company, Inc., 1943).
   A carefully selected series of research summaries on significant phases of child development, written by authorities in each area. Suitable for the more advanced student.
5. BERNARD, Harold W., *Adolescent Development in American Culture* (Yonkers, N. Y., World Book Company, 1957).
   One of the most recent texts, emphasizing the influence of the culture upon the adolescent.
6. BLAIR, Arthur Witt, and BURTON, William H., *Growth and Development of the Preadolescent* (New York, Appleton-Century-Crofts, Inc., 1951).
   Helpful for parents and teachers. The authors point out that this age is relatively neglected in literature and in research.

They offer principles and suggestions for help in guiding preadolescents.

7. BRECKENRIDGE, Marian E., and VINCENT, E. Lee, *Child Development: Physical and Psychologic Growth Through the School Years*, 3rd ed. (Philadelphia, W. B. Saunders Company, 1955).
The various aspects of development and the factors which influence them.

8. COOK, Lloyd Allen, *A Sociological Approach to Education* (New York, McGraw-Hill Book Company, Inc., 1950).
Summarizes several studies showing the influence of the culture on behavior. Points out implications for home, school, and community.

9. *Fostering Mental Health in our Schools*, Yearbook, Association for Supervision and Curriculum Development (Washington, D. C., National Education Association, 1950).
A series of excellent articles, generally in popular style, covering child development, and behavior in general. A brief and effective discussion of developmental tasks.

10. GESELL, Arnold, and ILG, Frances L., *Child Development; An Introduction to the Study of Human Growth* (New York, Harper and Brothers, 1949).
Includes two books: *Infant and Child in the Culture of Today* (covering the first five years), and *The Child from Five to Ten*. A useful text or reference book covering characteristics of the first ten years, setting forth explanations of behavior, and offering counsel to those who work and live with children. Based on Gesell's pioneering researches, these books are landmarks in the literature on characteristics of children. Rich in detail, attractive reading for layman and expert. Often criticized for basing results on a small group of children of above average socio-economic status.

11. GESELL, Arnold, et al., *The First Five Years of Life; A Guide to the Study of the Preschool Child* (New York, Harper and Brothers, 1940).
A detailed normative study of the preschool child. The methods involved in the study are described. Includes a useful pictorial survey. The first four chapters develop a point of view and summarize the characteristics of each stage.

12. GESELL, Arnold, ILG, Frances L., and AMES, Louise B., *Youth, The Years from Ten to Sixteen* (New York, Harper and Brothers, 1956).

Well written, offering a wealth of useful detail. Suffers from the admitted limitation of the selection of the subjects, around one hundred youth in New Haven, average IQ 117, half of them with fathers in the professions.

13. HAVIGHURST, Robert J., *Human Development and Education* (New York, Longmans, Green and Company, 1953).
    A study of the development of children in the light of their developmental tasks. Stresses the contribution of educational sociology.

14. HORROCKS, John E., *The Psychology of Adolescence* (Boston. Houghton Mifflin Company, 1951).
    One of the standard texts. A fairly conventional framework, as indicated by chapters on intellectual development, physical growth, motor abilities, interests, and social adjustment. The final chapter is an extended case history of a girl with a problem. Many summaries of pertinent research.

15. JENKINS, Gladys Gardner, SHACTER, Helen, and BAUER, William W., *These Are Your Children*: Expanded Edition (Chicago, Scott, Foresman and Company, 1953).
    Systematically follows the child stage by stage from birth through adolescence. Many characteristics identified, many descriptions of specific children, and many excellent photographs.

16. JERSILD, Arthur T., *Child Psychology*, 4th ed. (Englewood Cliffs, N. J., Prentice-Hall, Inc., 1954).
    A standard and highly popular text. Although conventional topics are included, there is also a great deal of attention given to the child's concept of himself.

17. ———, *The Psychology of Adolescence* (New York, The Macmillan Company, 1957).
    More than usual attention given to the "inner life" of adolescents, with four chapters on emotional development, three on social relationships, and one on fantasies and dreams.

18. KUHLEN, Raymond G., *The Psychology of Adolescent Development* (New York, Harper and Brothers, 1952).
    Somewhat more comprehensive but otherwise like Horrocks in its use of conventional topics and summarized research. Regards adolescence as "overdramatized," not unusually stressful, and not characterized by a "unique" psychology. Stresses relationships of the period to childhood and to adulthood.

19. MARTIN, William E., and STENDLER, Celia Burns, *Child Develop-*

ment: The Process of Growing Up in Society (New York, Harcourt, Brace and Company, Inc., 1953).

Emphasizes socialization, the mutual adaptation of the child and his society. A great deal of material from sociology and anthropology.

20. MARTIN, William E., and STENDLER, Celia Burns, *Readings in Child Development* (New York, Harcourt, Brace and Company, Inc., 1954).

An interdisciplinary approach to child development, stressing the contributions of the sociologist and anthropologist. In general, the papers are unabridged. An examination of the many forces influencing the developing behavior of the child as he advances to maturity.

21. MERRY, Frieda Kiefer, and MERRY, Ralph Vickers, *The First Two Decades of Life* (New York, Harper and Brothers, 1950).

A general textbook on child development. Devoted to explaining the "how" of the development of aspects of behavior such as motor, emotional, and social activities.

22. MILLARD, Cecil V., *Child Growth and Development in the Elementary School Years* (Boston, D. C. Heath and Company, 1951).

Examines the theories relating to many aspects of growth. No attempt at detailed description of children at each stage. Stimulating examination of current research in several areas as, for example, the interrelationships among the various phases of development.

23. MUNN, Norman L., *The Evolution and Growth of Human Behavior* (Boston, Houghton Mifflin Company, 1955).

A thorough and theoretical review of present knowledge about the psychology of growth and development. All but the last chapter are concerned primarily with the years from birth through middle childhood.

24. MUSSEN, Paul Henry, and CONGER, John Janeway, *Child Development and Personality* (New York, Harper and Brothers, 1956).

Emphasizing the concepts of learning and of personality development, this book is organized around the prenatal period, the first two years, the preschool years, middle childhood, and adolescence.

25. OLSON, Willard C., *Child Development* (Boston, D. C. Heath and Company, 1949).

An excellent general text setting forth the broad principles governing growth and development. Extensive reference to research available at that time.

26. PRESSEY, Sidney L., and KUHLEN, Raymond G., *Psychological Development Through the Life Span* (New York, Harper and Brothers, 1957).

    Differs from Munn (see above) in that attention is not concentrated on the early years. Offers more sociological data, less theoretical psychology.

27. REYNOLDS, Martha May, *Children From Seed to Saplings*, 2nd ed. (New York, McGraw-Hill Book Company, Inc., 1951).

    Many suggestions for both parents and teachers. Informal and nontechnical. Covers all ages to seventeen years, describing one age group at a time.

28. STEWART, Robert S., and WORKMAN, Arthur D., *Children and Other People: Achieving Maturity Through Learning* (New York, The Dryden Press, 1956).

    Brief, clearly written, less "textbookish" than most in this list. Treatment of stages of development and of common problems should be useful for layman and specialist.

29. STRANG, Ruth, *An Introduction to Child Study*, 3rd ed. (New York, The Macmillan Company, 1952).

    Both parents and teachers have found this book of value in learning about children. Organized by developmental stages. Covers behavior through the twentieth year, though the great emphasis is on the first thirteen years.

30. THORPE, Louis P., *Child Psychology and Development*, 2nd ed. (New York, The Ronald Press Company, 1955).

    The author, also a writer on mental hygiene, uses a broad, eclectic approach to child development.

31. WATTENBERG, William W., *The Adolescent Years* (New York, Harcourt, Brace and Company, 1955).

    Though somewhat repetitious, an excellent text for its emphasis on the feelings, motives, and perceptions of the adolescent. Employs many brief thumbnail sketches of adolescents.

Appendix IV

REPORTS AND SUMMARIES OF RESEARCH ON CHILD DEVELOPMENT

The following reports have been extensively used in developing the lists of characteristics in this book. Several books in Appendix III, notably those by Gesell, are essentially reports and summaries of research though they have been also widely used as texts and are therefore listed in that section.

1. *Adolescence*, 43rd Yearbook, National Society for the Study of Education, Part I. (Chicago, The University of Chicago Press, 1944).

    An outstanding collection of articles by experts on various phases of adolescence.

2. *Adolescent Girls, a Nation-wide Study of Girls Between Eleven and Eighteen Years of Age*, Survey Research Center (Ann Arbor, University of Michigan Press, 1956).

    This investigation was based on interviews conducted in 1955 with 1,925 girls, a representative national cross section drawn from all girls between eleven and eighteen years old who were in the sixth through the twelfth grades. Sixty-six sampling areas throughout the U. S. were used. Major topics include hopes, fears, plans, family relationships, friendship and dating, activities and interests, group membership, and contrasts between boys and girls.

3. BARKER, Roger G., and WRIGHT, Herbert F., *Midwest and Its Children* (Evanston, Illinois, Row, Peterson and Company, 1954).

4. *Encyclopedia of Educational Research*, Walter S. Monroe, editor (New York, The Macmillan Company, 1950).

    Comprehensive reports under headings: Child Development, Youth, Adolescence.

5. HORROCKS, John E., "The Adolescent," in L. Carmichael, editor, *Manual of Child Psychology*, 2nd edition (New York, John Wiley and Sons, Inc., 1954).

    An excellent summary of research.

6. *How Children Develop* (Columbus, The Ohio State University Press, 1949).

A valuable summary of behavior characteristics from later infancy through adolescence. Organized around four basic tasks facing children at all stages.

7. KINSEY, A. C., POMEROY, W. B., and MARTIN, C. E., *Sexual Behavior in the Human Male* (Philadelphia, W. B. Saunders Company, 1948).

8. ———, *Sexual Behavior in the Human Female* (Philadelphia, W. B. Saunders Company, 1953).

9. REMMERS, H. H., and RADLER, D. H., *The American Teenager* (Indianapolis, The Bobbs-Merrill Company, Inc., 1957).
Sums up the results of nation-wide surveys of attitudes of high school youth, conducted by Dr. Remmers from 1948 to the present.

10. *Research Relating to Children*, Children's Bureau, Clearinghouse for Research in Child Life, U. S. Department of Health, Education and Welfare, Washington, D. C. Issued periodically. Covers the most significant research in progress. Many studies deal with growth and development. For each study it covers the objectives, methods, principal researchers, period of study, and probable method of reporting.

11. SEARS, Robert R., MACCOBY, Eleanor E., and LEVIN, Harry, *Patterns of Child Rearing* (Evanston, Illinois, Row, Peterson and Company, 1957).
A study of how 379 American mothers brought up their children to kindergarten age.

12. STOLZ, H. R., and L. M., *Somatic Development of Adolescent Boys* (New York, The Macmillan Company, 1951).

13. *A Study of Adolescent Boys*, Survey Research Center (New Brunswick, New Jersey, Boy Scouts of America, 1956).
This investigation, conducted in 1954 by the Survey Research Center of the University of Michigan, was based on extended interviews with a sample of 1,045 subjects, drawn from all boys in the U. S. who were in the ages fourteen through sixteen and were attending public school between the seventh and twelfth grades. Thirty-four sampling areas were used.

The Society for Research in Child Development, Washington, D.C., is a major source of research reports. They are available through Child Development Publications, Purdue University, Lafayette, Indiana. The Society has three publications:

14. *Child Development Abstracts and Bibliography*, three issues each year.

APPENDIX IV

15. *Child Development*, a quarterly.
16. *Monographs of the Society for Research in Child Development.*

The following monographs have been of particular value in the preparation of this booklet:

17. GREULICH, W. W., et al., *Somatic and Endocrine Studies of Puberal and Adolescent Boys*, 1942.
18. SHUTTLEWORTH, F. K., *The Adolescent Period*, 1938. of elementary school children. Gives insight into both the nature of children and the school's program.
19. ———, *The Adolescent Period: A Pictorial Atlas*, 1949.
20. ———, *Sexual Maturation and the Physical Growth of Girls, Ages Six to Nineteen*, 1937.
21. SIMMONS, K., *The Brush Foundation Study of Child Growth and Development*, Part II, 1944.

Other useful annuals and periodicals reporting research in child development are:

22. *Annual Review of Psychology.*
23. *Child Development Monographs.*
24. *Genetic Psychology Monographs.*
25. *Journal of Genetic Psychology.*
26. *Review of Educational Research* (Issue on growth and development every three years).

Occasionally general research journals have reports on child development. The following is a good example:

27. GRAY, George W., "Human Growth," *Scientific American* (October, 1953), pp. 65-74.

Appendix V

GENERAL BOOKS, PAMPHLETS, AND JOURNALS ON CHILD DEVELOPMENT

Inexpensive Books

The following six books have several features in common. They are paperbacks, available at 35 cents each. They are written for both the parent and the teacher. They emphasize practical problems met by adults who are helping children grow up. They are well written and will be read with enjoyment.

1. Arnold, Arnold, *How to Play with your Child* (New York, Ballantine Books, 1955).

    The author, an artist and designer of children's toys, offers many helpful ideas and suggestions on topics such as the appropriateness of toys and kinds of play for various ages. The play possibilities in art, music, and learning are described and related to such things as individual play, creative play, and unsupervised play.

2. Duncan, Eleanor S., *Baby Care: A Mother's Guide to the First Six Years* (New York, Lion Books, Inc., 1955).

    Originally published by McGraw-Hill. Copyright 1952 by Parents' Institute, Inc. Follows the child in nine age stages through kindergarten.

3. Edwards, Morton, ed., *Your Child From 2 to 5* (New York, Permabooks, 1955).

    In the words of the editor it is "a reporter's pad crammed with jottings of interest to parents of young children." Many articles, bulletins, and reports dealing with matters of interest to parents and teachers have been summarized in a useful manner.

4. Frank, Mary, and Lawrence K., *How to Help Your Child in School* (New York, New American Library of World Literature, Inc., 1950).

    A reprint of the original hard cover edition published by the Viking Press, Inc. Discussion of the characteristics, by stages,

5. ILG, Frances L., and AMES, Louise B., *Child Behavior* (New York, Dell Publishing Company, Inc., 1955).
   This book is also available from Harper and Brothers, New York, 1955. Written by co-workers of Dr. Arnold Gesell. Offers help in understanding children in the first ten years. Examples of chapter headings: "Eating Behavior," "Sleeping and Dreams," "Elimination," "Fears," and "Brothers and Sisters."
6. SPOCK, Benjamin, *The Pocket Book of Baby and Child Care* 2nd ed. (New York, Pocket Books, Inc., 1957).
   Helps with the understanding of children's problems from babyhood through puberty.

The next two books are by James L. Hymes, Jr. (New York, Prentice-Hall, Inc., 1955). They are cloth-bound ($2.25), attractively made, and brief. They are written for the teacher but will give the parent a new understanding of the role of the school and a new appreciation of it. Within a few pages the author captures the best in modern education.

7. *A Child Development Point of View*. Built around three themes —your youngster must like you, their work, themselves.
8. *Behavior and Misbehavior: A Teacher's Guide to Action*. Discipline for the normal and for the disturbed child under the limiting conditions generally faced by teachers.

The following books help clarify the role of the culture in determining children's behavior.

9. DAVIS, W. Allison, and HAVIGHURST, Robert J., *Father of the Man: How Your Child Gets His Personality* (Boston, Houghton Mifflin Company, 1947).
10. MEAD, Margaret, *Coming of Age in Samoa* (New York, New American Library of World Literature, Inc., 1949).
    A Mentor Book, 35 cents. First published in 1928 by William Morrow and Company.
11. MEAD, Margaret, *Growing Up in New Guinea* (New York, New American Library of World Literature, Inc., 1953).
    A Mentor Book, 35 cents. First published in 1930 by William Morrow and Company.
12. WARNER, W. L., HAVIGHURST, R. J., and LOEB, M. B., *Who Shall Be Educated?* (New York, Harper and Brothers, 1944).
13. WARNER, W. L., MEEKER, M., and EELLS, K., *Social Class in America* (Chicago, Science Research Associates, 1949).

Pamphlets

Many organizations publish useful pamphlets on various phases of child development which are useful for parents and teachers. All are nominally priced or free. Some of the most useful of these pamphlets are listed below.

Association for Childhood Education International, 1200 Fifteenth Street, N.W., Washington 5, D.C. While the publications of this organization tend to feature life in school they are of much value to parents. Typical are the following.

14. GESELL, Arnold, and others, "About Children—How They Learn, Feel, and Grow," 50 cents.
15. MIEL, Alice, and others, "Guiding Children in School and Out," 1953. 50 cents.
16. NETERER, Elizabeth, ed. "Helping Children Grow," 1951. $1.25.

Association for Supervision and Curriculum Development, 1201 Sixteenth Street, N.W., Washington 6, D.C. Many books and pamphlets dealing with phases of the growth and development of children, generally from the teacher's point of view. Typical is the following excellent pamphlet by George Sheviakov and Fitz Redl.

17. "Discipline for Today's Children and Youth," 1944. 50 cents.

Better Living Booklets, Science Research Associates, 228 S. Wabash Avenue, Chicago 4, Illinois. "Intended to help parents, teachers, and others concerned with the development of children to do a better job of their challenging task." This has been done in a series of pamphlets of which the following are especially helpful. 40 cents.

18. NEISSER, Edith G., "How to Live with Children," 1950.
19. THURSTONE, Thelma G., and BYRNE, Katharine M., "Mental Abilities of Children," 1951.

Committee on Mental Health, State Charities Aid Association, 105 East 22nd Street, New York 10, New York. A series of brief, ten-cent pamphlets dealing with specific problems in child development.

20. "When a Child Has Fears."
21. "When a Child Is Destructive."
22. "When a Child Masturbates."

APPENDIX V 107

Freedom Pamphlets, Anti-Defamation League of B'nai B'rith, 212 Fifth Avenue, New York 10, New York. Pamphlets throwing light on the development of basic concepts in children. Most useful is the following by Howard A. Lane.

23. "Shall Children, too, Be Free?" 1949. 25 cents.

Health Education Service; Life Conservation Service, John Hancock Mutual Life Insurance Company, Boston, Massachusetts. This series, developed by experts in the field, covers many aspects of the growth and development of children. Available free upon request.

24. "Between One and Five," 1950.
25. "From Six to Twelve," 1953.
26. "In the Teens," 1953.
27. "Your Child Grows Up," 1953.

Life Adjustment Booklets, Science Research Associates, Inc., 57 W. Grand Avenue, Chicago 10, Illinois. 40 cents. Written for young people but well worth reading by parents also. An instructor's guide is available for use by the teacher.

28. KIRKENDALL, Lester A., "Understanding Sex," 1947.
29. SHACTER, Helen, "Getting Along with Others," 1949.
30. WEITZMAN, Ellis, "Growing Up Socially," 1949.

Metropolitan Life Insurance Company, Home Office: New York; Pacific Coast Office: San Francisco. Many titles available free upon request. The following are of particular value.

31. "Common Childhood Diseases." (Pictures included to aid in diagnosing sickness.) 1953.
32. "Understanding Your Young Child," 1954.
33. "What Teachers See," 1952.

National Mental Health Foundation, 1520 Race Street, Philadelphia 2, Pennsylvania.

34. RIDENOUR, Nina and JOHNSON, Isabel, "Some Special Problems of Children Ages 2 to 5 Years," 1949. 25 cents.
35. HYMES, James L., Jr., "Teacher Listen—The Children Speak," 1949. 25 cents.

Parent-Teacher Series, Bureau of Publications, Teachers College, Columbia University. Useful books of which the following are a good example. 60 cents each.

36. HYMES, James L., Jr., "Discipline," 1949.
37. MAYER, Jane, "Getting Along in the Family," 1949.

Public Affairs Pamphlets, Published by the Public Affairs Committee, Inc., 22 East 38th Street, New York 16, New York. Excellent reading for both adults and young people. The following titles are closely related to matters discussed in this book. 25 cents each.

38. DUVALL, Evelyn, "Keeping up with Teen-Agers," 1947.
39. HYMES, James L., "Enjoy Your Child—Ages 1, 2, and 3," 1948.
40. ———, "Three to Six: Your Child Starts to School," 1950.
41. LAMBERT, Clara, "Understand Your Child—From 6 to 12," 1948.
42. LANDIS, Paul H., "Coming of Age: Problems of Teen Agers."

U. S. Government Pamphlets, Government Printing Office, Washington 25, D. C. The number of helpful government pamphlets about the behavior and development of children is very large.

43. "Your Child, a Must List for Parents," in which 24 of the most popular publications covering child care from birth to the middle 'teens are listed. 1957. Other government titles include the following.
44. GABBARD, Hazel F., "Preparing Your Child for School," 1949. 15 cents.
45. "Your Child from One to Six," 1956. 20 cents.
46. "Your Child from Six to Twelve," 1949. 20 cents.
47. "The Adolescent in Your Family," 1955. 25 cents.
48. SEGEL, David, "Intellectual Abilities in the Adolescent Period," 1948. 15 cents.

JOURNALS

There are several excellent journals and magazines that contribute to understanding of child development. The following are recommended.

49. *California Parent-Teacher,* 322 West 21st Street, Los Angeles 7, California. $1.25 a year. Monthly except July. Other state P.T.A.'s have similar magazines.
50. *Child Study,* Published quarterly by the Child Study Association of America, details from State Department of Education, 132 East 74th Street, New York 21, New York. $2.50 a year. Written for the more sophisticated parent and the teacher.
51. *Children,* Published bi-monthly by the U. S. Department of Health, Education, and Welfare. $1.25 a year. "An interdisciplinary journal for the professions serving children."

APPENDIX V

Many articles would be of interest for the general reader. Available through the Government Printing Office, Washington 25, D. C.

52. *Childhood Education,* The Association for Childhood Education International, 1200 15th Street, N.W., Washington 5, D. C. $4.50 a year. Nine issues per year. Articles are short and generally not technical. Several in each issue are focussed on one selected theme. Useful for the layman as well as teachers concerned with children from two to twelve.
53. *National Parent-Teacher,* 600 S. Michigan Boulevard, Chicago 5, Illinois. $1.25 a year. Monthly, September through June.
54. *Parents' Magazine,* 52 Vanderbilt Avenue, New York 17, New York. $3.00 a year. Monthly.
55. *Understanding the Child,* National Association for Mental Health, 1790 Broadway, New York, New York. $1.50 a year. Quarterly. More useful for the professional worker.

Appendix VI

FILMS ON CHILD DEVELOPMENT

The films listed below have been found useful by both college and community study groups. Unless otherwise indicated all are in black and white and with sound tracks.

These films are generally available in the film libraries of school districts, county offices, state departments of education, and colleges. They may be ordered directly from the sources indicated in the annotations. The address of each source is shown the first time it appears in the list.

1. *Age of Turmoil.* McGraw-Hill Book Company, Text-Film Department, 330 West 42nd Street, New York 18, New York. 20 minutes. 1952.

    Depicts the emotional turmoil of the early teen-ager. Three boys and three girls illustrate varying kinds of problems, degrees of maturity, and home environments.

Ages and Stages Films. The following series of films was developed by Crawley Films of Canada for the National Film Board and is distributed in the United States by McGraw-Hill Book Company. The stages identified in this Canadian film check closely with research conducted here. Children are shown in a variety of situations both in and out of school. The films are interesting and instructive. The commentary leads to understanding of the behavior being observed and suggests ways for parents and teachers to enjoy and help children.

2. *Terrible Twos and Trusting Threes.* 20 minutes. 1950. Color.
3. *Frustrating Fours and Fascinating Fives.* 22 minutes. 1952. Color.
4. *From Sociable Six to Noisy Nine.* 22 minutes. 1954. Color.
5. *From Ten to Twelve.* 26 minutes. 1956.
6. *The Teens.* 26 minutes. 1956.
7. *Children Growing up with Other People.* Educational Film Department, United World Films, Inc., 7356 Melrose Avenue, Hollywood 46, California. 30 minutes. 1948. British film showing how children adapt to changing conditions as they mature.

APPENDIX VI

8. *Discovering Individual Differences.* McGraw-Hill Book Company. 25 minutes. 1954. (Follows *Each Child is Different.*)

    Shows how the teacher studied the children in the first film using the following techniques: observations, cumulative records, behavior journals, discussions with other teachers and parents, and a staff conference.

9. *Each Child Is Different.* McGraw-Hill Book Company, 17 minutes. 1954. (Followed by *Discovering Individual Differences.*)

    Shows the home and community influences on the lives of five children in a fifth grade class. The teacher realizes that if she is to be effective with these children she must understand them.

10. *He Acts His Age.* McGraw-Hill Book Company. 15 minutes. 1951. Color.

    Follows the changing patterns of behavior of children through the fifteenth year as illustrated in play situations.

11. *Helping Teachers to Understand Children.* United World Films, Inc. Two parts: 21 minutes and 25 minutes. 1946.

    Guide to child study groups organized by the University of Maryland but of value to any child study group.

12. *Human Growth.* E. C. Brown Trust, 220 S.W. Adler Street, Portland 4, Oregon. 20 minutes. 1948.

    A seventh grade class views a film tracing life from embryo to maturity. Structural differences between male and female discussed. Interesting both for general information conveyed and for the reactions of children in discussion of what they have seen.

13. *Life with Baby.* McGraw-Hill Book Company. 18 minutes. 1949.

    March of Time. Dr. Gesell (then director of the Yale University Clinic of Child Development) and his associates examine children in the clinic so as to show characteristic behaviors at various ages within the first year as well as at ages two and three. Parts of a simple test of intelligence are demonstrated. The film emphasizes the importance of understanding what are typical behaviors and the need of each child to proceed at his own pace.

14. *Life with Junior.* McGraw-Hill Book Company. 18 minutes. 1949.

    A ten-year-old boy dawdles and forgets his schedule, has good manner when he remembers, shows increasing independence of parents, is a heavy eater, reads the comics devotedly.

Parents reveal their anxieties about his development, and the film suggests ways to cope with his behavior.

15. *Meaning of Adolescence.* McGraw-Hill Book Company. 20 minutes. 1953.

    The induction into manhood status of a fourteen-year-old boy in a primitive tribe is contrasted with the prolonged transition between puberty and adulthood in our society. Five needed adjustments of adolescents are cited. The film finally contrasts two adolescents, a boy whose parents do not understand this age, and a girl whose parents provide needed help and guidance.

16. *Meeting Emotional Needs in Children.* New York University Film Library, 26 Washington Pl., New York 3, New York. 1947.

    Relates basic emotional needs to "laying the ground work for democracy." Scenes in home, school, and community. Changing pattern of needs as children mature. Guides for both parents and teachers.

17. *Meeting the Needs of Adolescents.* McGraw-Hill Book Company. 19 minutes. 1953.

    Revolving around a fourteen-year-old boy and his seventeen-year-old sister, the film demonstrates the physical, mental, spiritual, and social needs of adolescents.

18. *Physical Aspects of Puberty.* McGraw-Hill Book Company. 20 minutes. 1947.

    Describes the glandular processes and the resultant primary and secondary sexual developments of boys and girls during puberty. Gives examples of the impact of early and late development upon both sexes.

19. *Preface to a Life.* United World Films, Inc. 29 minutes. 1950.

    Illustrates what might happen to a child if the parents try to shape him according to their images.

20. *Principles of Development.* McGraw-Hill Book Company. 17 minutes. 1950.

    Reviews the basic concepts in growth and development and then considers the factors leading to divergent behavior at each stage.

21. *Social Development.* McGraw-Hill Book Company. 16 minutes. 1950.

    Points out the characteristic social developments in infancy, then in the preschool years, and finally in the "gang age."

There are available from the Superintendent of Documents,

APPENDIX VI

Government Printing Office, Washington 25, D.C. three booklets which list many films relating to child development. Running time, sources, and other necessary information are given.

22. *Motion Pictures on Child Life.* 1952. 40 cents.
23. *Supplement 1 to Motion Pictures on Child Life.* 1954. 15 cents.
24. *Supplement 2 to Motion Pictures on Child Life.* 1956. 15 cents.

Index

Accidents, in early adolescence, 72
Acne, 72
Adolescence:
   early, *see* Early adolescence
   "first," 33
   late, *see* Late adolescence
Adolescent, meaning of term, 79
Aggression, 27, 38
Allowances and earnings, 43, 55, 65
Anger, 61
Anxiety, 27, 73-74
Arithmetic learning, 42
Art and creative interests, 30-31, 51, 55, 66
Attention span, 53, 65

Baseball, 63
Behavior:
   developmental stages, *see* Development, stages in
   forward and continuous aspects, 10,
   from generalized to specific, 10
   irregularity of, 11
   "typical," 15-16
   see also separate developmental stages
Behavior problems, 25-27, 36-38, 46, 49-50, 56-57, 61-62, 69, 73-74
Bluebirds, 39
Boasting, 38
Bone development, 24, 59
Boy-girl comparative development, 24, 28, 38, 42, 46, 51, 58, 63, 76
Brain development, 34, 64, 80
Brownies, 39
Bullying, 56

California, University of, 2
Caloric needs, 47, 59, 71-72
Campfire Girls, 76

Cheating, 36, 83
Child Development (Gesell), 1
Child Development Laboratory, Michigan State University, 2
Children, *passim:*
   basic developmental principles, 9-13
   developmental characteristics, *see* Development *and* separate developmental stages
   differences in, 6-9
   sameness in, 1-6
Church attendance, 67, 83
Church organizations, 76
Clubs, 39, 76
Collecting, 54, 66
College, 86, 90
Columbia University, 2
Comic books, 42
Conscience, 32, 66
Creative expression, *see* Art and creative interests
"Crowd," the, 62
Cruelty, 49

Dancing, 35, 77
Dating, 74, 77, 87, 90
Davis, Allison, 2
Daydreaming, 50, 66
Death attitudes, 45, 57
Death causes, in early adolescence, 72
Delinquency, 56, 62, 79
Depression, 50
Development:
   sequence of, 12-13
   stages in, 3, 16-19, 21-22, 33-34, 46-47, 58-59, 68-70, 85-86
   see also separate stages
Developmental task, defined, 3-4
Discouragement, 50
Disease, 24, 33, 35
Draft, 86

INDEX

Early adolescence, 18, 68-84
  emotional development, 73-74
  mental development, 80-83
  moral and spiritual development, 83
  physical development, 70-71
  social development, 74-79
Early childhood, 17, 33-45
  emotional development, 36-38
  mental development, 40-43
  moral and spiritual development, 43-45
  physical development, 34-35
  social development, 38-40
Economic influences, 52
Eight-year-olds, *see* Early childhood
Eighteen-year-olds, *see* Late adolescence
Eleven-year-olds, (boys), *see* Later childhood
Eleven-year-olds (girls), *see* Preadolescence
Emotional development, 7
  in early adolescence, 73-74
  in early childhood, 36-38
  in infancy, 24-27
  in late adolescence, 86
  in later childhood, 48-50
  preadolescent, 60-62
Environment, 3, 8
"Eraser stage," 43
Eyes, 22, 34-35, 47

Family, child's dependence on, 24-25, 28-29, 36, 39-40, 52, 54, 61, 63, 77-79, 88
Father, child's dependence on, 28
Fears, 37, 50, 61
Fifteen-year-olds, *see* Early adolescence
Five-year-olds, *see* Infancy
Football, 63
Foreign language learning, 42
Four-year-olds, *see* Infancy
Fourteen-year-olds, *see* Early adolescence
Friendship, 38, 63, 74-75
Frustration, 26, 61

Games, 48, 63
  see also Play
Gangs, 39, 50, 56, 62
Gesell, Arnold, 1, 2
Girl-boy comparative development, 24, 28, 38, 42, 46, 51, 58, 63, 76
Girl Scouts, 76
Gland development, 72
Going steady, 77, 87-88
Group adjustments, 29, 33, 38-39, 51, 76
Growth, 34, 47
  inter-relationships, 11
  patterns of, 12, 16-17
  see also Emotional development *and* Physical development
Guilt feelings, 83

Handedness, 23
Havighurst, Robert J., 2, 3-4
Harvard University, 2
Health, 24, 35, 47-48, 50, 59, 71-73
Heart, 34, 48
Height characteristics, 92-95
Heredity, 4, 7, 8
Hero worship, 53, 83
Home responsibilities, 43, 52, 56, 66
Humor, 40, 55, 80

Indian Guides, 39
Infancy (first five years), 2-32
  emotional development, 24-27
  mental development, 29-31
  moral and spiritual development, 31-32
  physical development, 22-24
  social development, 27-29
Intelligence quotient (IQ), 6, 8, 12, 13
Iowa Child Welfare Research Station, 2

Jealousy, 29

Kindergarten, 21
Kinsey, A. C., 72

INDEX

Late adolescence, 18-19, 85-90
  emotional development, 86
  mental development, 88-90
  moral and spiritual development, 90
  physical development, 86
  social development, 87-88
Later childhood, 17, 46-57
  emotional development, 48-50
  mental development, 53-55
  moral and spiritual development, 55-57
  physical development, 47-48
  social development, 50-53
Leadership, 39
Leisure activities, 80-81
  see also Play
Lying, 36, 56

Marriage interest, 81, 82, 85-89
Masturbation, 27, 72
Mead, Margaret, 2, 8
Menstruation, 58, 73, 74
  onset of, 94-95
Mental age, 13
Mental development:
  in early adolescence, 80-83
  in early childhood, 40-43
  in infancy, 29-31
  in late adolescence, 88-90
  in later childhood, 53-55
  preadolescent, 64-66
Michigan State University, 2
Millard, Cecil V., 2
Moral and spiritual development:
  in early adolescence, 83
  in early childhood, 43-45
  in infancy, 31-32
  in late adolescence, 90
  in later childhood, 55-57
  preadolescent, 66-67
Mother, child's dependence on, 24, 28
Motor age, 13
Muscle development, 23-24, 35, 47, 59, 71
Musical ability, 41

Negativism, 26
Nine-year-olds, *see* Later childhood

Nineteen-year-olds, *see* Late adolescence

One-year-olds, see Infancy

Parents, 5-6, 9
  see also Family, Father, *and* Mother
Part-time work, 82-83, 90
Peers, 27-28, 29, 38-39, 48, 50-51, 62-63, 68, 74-77
Pets, 42-43
Physical development, 3, 6
  in early adolescence, 70-71
  in early childhood, 34-35
  in infancy, 22-24
  in late adolescence, 86
  in later childhood, 47-48
  preadolescent, 59-60
Play, 24, 28, 31, 35, 39, 42, 54, 66
Posture, 35, 47-48, 59, 71
Prayers, 44, 67
Preadolescence, 17-18, 58-67
  emotional development, 60-62
  mental development, 64-66
  moral and spiritual development, 66-67
  physical development, 59-60
  social development, 62-64
Pregnancy, 73
Prejudices, 51
Pubertal development, 17, 94-95

Racial attitudes, 38, 50
Readiness, pupil, 5, 42
Reading ability, 42, 54, 65
Reading interests, 31, 42, 53, 54, 66, 81
Regression, 26
Religion, *see* Moral and spiritual development
Research, 2, 3, 13-16, 19
Rhythmic activities, 35, 41
Rockefeller Institute of Child Welfare, 2
Rural-life groups, 76

INDEX

School organizations, 76
Scouts, 63, 76
Self-consciousness, 73-74
Seven-year-olds, *see* Early childhood
Seventeen-year-olds, *see* Late adolescence
Sex development, 28, 35, 38, 42, 52, 58, 70, 72-73, 74, 79, 94-95
Shyness, 37-38
Six-year-olds, *see* Early Childhood
Sixteen-year-olds (boys), *see* Early adolescence
Sixteen-year-olds (girls), *see* Late adolescence
Sleep, 24, 35, 48, 59, 72
Social development, 3-4, 7, 8
   in early adolescence, 74-79
   in early childhood, 38-40
   in infancy, 27-29
   in late adolescence, 87-88
   in later childhood, 50-53
   preadolescent, 62-64
Stanford University, 2
Stealing, 36, 56, 66
Stolz, Herbert, 16
Sunday school, 44, 67

Tattling, 32, 40
Teacher, child's dependence on, 4-5, 9, 36, 38, 39-40, 53, 63-64, 79
Team games, 51, 80
Teamwork, 63
"Teen-ager," 79

Teeth, 22, 34, 59, 72
Temper, 24
Ten-year-olds, *see* Later childhood
Thirteen-year-olds (boys), *see* Preadolescence
Thirteen-year-olds (girls), *see* Early adolescence
Three-year-olds, *see* Infancy
Thumb sucking, 27, 37
Time concept, 40
Truancy, 50
Twelve-year-olds, *see* Preadolescence
Twenty-year-olds, *see* Late Adolescence
Two-year-olds, *see* Infancy

Vocabulary, 26, 29-30, 54
Vocation interests, 55, 81-83, 86, 88-89

Warner, Lloyd W., 2, 8
Weight characteristics, 92-95
Withdrawal, 49
Writing, 42, 66

Yale Institute of Human Development, 1
Youth, the Years from Ten to Sixteen (Gesell), 1
Y. M. C. A., 63, 76
Y. W. C. A., 76